6/16/14

Susan:

May the Lord Reward
You As you Continue to Do
Service to Others!

Mother P. Gentry

In the Closet of Prayer

St. Matthew 6:6- But thou, when thou prayest, enter into thy closet, and when thou hast shut thy door, pray to thy Father which is in secret; and thy Father which seeth in secret shall reward thee openly. (KJV)

MOTHER PAULINE GENTRY

WestBow·
PRESS
A DIVISION OF THOMAS NELSON
& ZONDERVAN

Scripture taken from the King James Version of the Bible.

WestBow Press books may be ordered through booksellers or by contacting:

WestBow Press
A Division of Thomas Nelson & Zondervan
1663 Liberty Drive
Bloomington, IN 47403
www.westbowpress.com
1 (866) 928-1240

ISBN: 978-1-4908-3400-9 (sc)
ISBN: 978-1-4908-3401-6 (hc)
ISBN: 978-1-4908-3399-6 (e)

Library of Congress Control Number: 2014907170

Printed in the United States of America.

WestBow Press rev. date: 05/01/2014

Contents

Appendices

Foreword

In the Closet of Prayer is a wonderful book that will inspire, encourage, and also motivate you to pray and see the awesome miracles God can perform through prayer. The Bible says that the effectual, fervent prayer of a righteous man or woman avails much (James 5:16).

Pauline Gentry, my mother, is a great example of this Scripture. She has devoted her life to prayer and spent many hours in the face of God, never wavering but faithful and believing.

My mother continues to be a woman of prayer, like Anna the prophetess, spending many hours in the church on the first pew, down on her knees, pouring out her heart to God.

Despite many challenges, she presses forward, knowing God can do anything but fail.

Pastor Tony Gentry

Preface

This book is written to let you know that the God of the Bible still works in the twenty-first century, performing miracles, signs, and wonders. You may be struggling with sickness and disease, addictions, strongholds, financial deprivation, depression, dysfunctional relationships, and so forth and need divine intervention. If so, this book is for you. Each chapter in this book is based on testimonies of personal experiences with God while *In the Closet of Prayer.*

Acknowledgments

First I want to thank and praise God for manifesting Himself to me in revelations, dreams, and visions in my daily walk with Him. Psalm 108:8 says, "Oh that men would praise the Lord for his goodness and for his wonderful works to the children of men!" Therefore I praise God for His excellent greatness and His miracles performed in the lives of men.

I thank Bishop J. C. Gilkey Sr. for the trust he has in me and the encouraging words he gave me when I expressed to him my desire to write this book. I appreciate him for his love, kindness, and prayers.

I thank my son Pastor Tony Gentry for his support and contribution to this book. I dedicate this book to him and my other children, Everett, Michelle, Marchelle, and Elias, and my grandchildren and great-granddaughter, Emaria Pauline.

A special thank you to my daughter Evangelist Carlotta Gentry, my sister, Dr. Charlene Hogan, my niece Minister Andrea Hogan, and friend Missionary Roshelyn McCoy for their input.

Thanks to all my supporters and contributors who gave me encouraging words and allowed me to add their names to this book.

My motto in life is, "If I can help somebody as I travel along this journey of prayer, then my living will not have been in vain." I love you all.

About the Author

My Early Childhood Years

I am the eleventh of twelve children, born on March 26, 1945. I was delivered by a midwife (Rosie McGhee) to Willie and Alice Hill in Hickory Grove, Arkansas, which is a small community located between the cities of Nashville and Lockesburg, Arkansas. Before I was born, my mother had problems during her childbirth, and they did not think one of us would live. The midwife asked my father during the delivery which one he wanted to save—me or my mother—and he said my mother, but God had another plan in mind. Not only was I delivered, but my mother lived also. She lived long enough to see me grown and married and deliver two of her grandchildren.

My parent were dedicated Christians and devoted their lives to the service of the Lord. My dad, Willie, was a preaching deacon and Sunday school superintendent. He would open the doors of the church in preparation for service. My mother, Alice, was a missionary, the church secretary/clerk, the treasurer of the Sunday school, and in charge of setting up communion. The Lord also revealed Himself to her in dreams and visions.

My parent sharecropped on someone else's land during my early-childhood years until 1952. They worked the land and plowed the fields. They seemed to be able to know the time to eat by watching the sun and would eat at noon under shade trees, where they *prayed* over and blessed the food.

Even though my parents worked hard in their early years, the hard work did not prevent them from going to church. We would go to church in wagons pulled by mules. The Lord later blessed my dad to buy a Model T Ford, and then he progressed to buying a car. In my early junior high school years, they had a new home built. I never experienced a lack of food or clothing. My parents learned the formula for survival by staying on their knees *In the Closet of Prayer*. Whether at home or at church, everyone was found on their knees in *prayer*.

Social Location

The Hickory Grove Church of God in Christ where I attended was the center of the community. It was the place of worship, the place where God's principles were taught and practiced. Almost everyone in the community went to church. Our church was a one-room white building with two little rooms on each side at the back.

We had no indoor plumbing. However, it did have electricity. It had hard wood floors (planks) that made music with the patting of the feet and every shout as the saints would go forth in dance. The pews were filled with homemade stuffed pillows to sit on, and they were placed on the floor when we *kneeled to pray*.

Our Sunday school would start at 9:30 a.m., but we had no particular time when our church service would start. We would sometimes go to church in the morning and stay all day until after the night service, taking a lunch and an evening snack. At the church there was a condiment stand where a man named Mr. Sylvester Baker sold pop, peanuts, candy, gum, etc. During the early years, most people would travel by horse and buggy or wagon.

For many years my parents would house the pastor and his family, providing for them a guest bedroom so they could stay when they would come to render services. My mother would cook for the pastors and evangelist who would travel there to preach or run revivals. I had a humbled beginning, but was blessed to be bought up in a home where good morals and right living were taught. My father often quoted the Scripture from Proverbs 14:34: "Righteousness exalteth a nation: but sin is a reproach to any people."

In the Closet of Prayer

The Vision

I was inspired to write this book after the Lord visited me in a dream. In the dream I was in the St. Mark Church of God in Christ in Wichita, Kansas, and I went to my pastor, Bishop J. C. Gilkey Sr., as he was talking to a group of people I did not recognize. I told him these people were vicious, and his reply to me was, "But I am not going to "take down" (change my point of view).

I decided I was going to get my things and leave. As I prepared to go out one entrance of the church, there were people on the outside pouring gasoline around the church to set it on fire. Therefore I decided I would go out the other entrance, and as I began to go out the other side of the church, there were people shooting people down on the outside. Therefore I proceeded to go to the finance room, where there was an exit to the south. In that room there was a table.

I looked at the table and thought about going underneath it and decided I couldn't go under it because I could be seen and there was not enough protection. I then saw a *closet.* I headed for *the closet,* hoping to find shelter in the closet. I then woke up. The next day I was in my home at the kitchen sink and was wondering why the closet was in the dream. Then it came to me: *In the Closet of Prayer.* Therefore I titled this book *In the Closet of Prayer.*

Matthew 6:6 says, *"But thou when thou, prayest, enter into thy closet,* and when thou hast shut thy door, pray to thy Father which is in secret; and thy Father which seeth in secret shall reward thee openly."

The Prophecy

Minister Alvin Mason prophesied to me that I was going to write a book when he was ministering in the pulpit at St. Mark Church of God in Christ in Wichita, Kansas. Pastor Mark L. Gilkey also prophesied this while he was praying in the same church. He walked over to me and said, "I see a book—a white book." He then stated, "Mother Dabney." He not only made a correlation between me and her then but also several years later. I did not fully understand the prophecy at the time, but I understood later, knowing that Mother E. J. Dabney was a great praying woman of God who the Lord used through her determination and effective prayer Life. She wrote a book entitled *What It Means to Pray Through.* I now have experienced this in my prayer life and will share in this book what it means to pray through! This book will help you realize God is the same yesterday, today, and forever.

In this book I will share visions and prophesies God has given to me in all aspects of my life, and I attribute a large part of it to my consistent prayer life. Prayer has helped me in this Christian journey to know that God is real, and He changes not.

Chapter 1

God's Revealing Nature

Testimony of Witness of a Call on My Life

On one occasion when I was an early teen, *two prophets,* one Caucasian and the other an African American, walked into our Little Hickory Grove Church late one night unannounced. When they were asked to address the church, they stated that they had come with *a prophecy* and were just being obedient to God. Then they sat down. After church was dismissed and we had returned home, we heard a knock on the door, and it was the prophets. When they entered our home, they said to my parents that they had a *prophecy* for one of their daughters and described me. There were other siblings at home, but they singled me out.

One ministered to me and said the Lord wanted to use me. The other one told me the same thing and added that I might marry someone and experience some difficult times in the relationship. The last thing they said to me that I could be afflicted with an incurable disease if I did not give my life to the Lord. Even after the prophecy, I did not surrender my life to the Lord at that time. Prior to my senior year in high school I gave my life to the Lord, but I later turned away from God or backslid.

Early Prophecy Fulfilled

For years I pondered those thoughts in my heart, and on April 12, 1965, I married Cordell Gentry while I was still out of fellowship with God. To this union two boys were born: Tony Untra Gentry, who is now a pastor, and Everett Lamon Gentry. As it was prophesied, we did experience some challenges in our marriage, but in the midst of the challenges, the good days outweighed the bad.

As years passed we separated from each other and later divorced. We remained friends, and he always referred to me as his wife because he knew the love I had for him and his family. He passed away in 1998.

Before he died, we stayed in close contact with one another, and at one point we talked about rekindling our relationship. At this time I had given my life back to the Lord. He came to Wichita, Kansas, where I was living after our separation, around 1985 and met my pastor, Bishop J. C. Gilkey Sr., who told me he thought Cordell was a nice man. Then I told the bishop that he and I had talked about getting back together. Bishop Gilkey said only five words to me: "If the Lord save him."

I decided I wanted more from God, and I began to seek God more. My ex-husband and I continued to communicate, but the more I sought the Lord in fasting and praying, the more my mind was elevated in the things of the Lord and less on rekindling a relationship with my ex-husband. Approximately one year after my pastor, Bishop Gilkey, had said, "If the Lord save him," I was a few yards from my home, and automatically said those same words.

Cordell and I continued to be in communication with each other, but we never rekindled our relationship. I later adopted my twin great-nieces, Michelle and Marchelle Moore, and he agreed that they would take on his last name of Gentry. My ex-husband passed away in June of 1998. He had a military home-going, and his family saw that I had all the rights and privileges of a soldier's wife.

Testimonies

Salvation and the Early Years of God's Revelations

Revelation 1

In 1961 in Frederick, Oklahoma, Elder Howard Huggins was my pastor. This was when the Lord first began to reveal to me His mysteries, soon after I received salvation. I knew the power of prayer by observing my parents. I had watched my mother pray and get results. I also watched the Lord reveal to my mother (aspiring missionary Alice Hill) His mysteries through dreams.

One of the first revelations of the Lord to me was in the '60s. I had a dream, which I shared with my sisters, Missionary Annette Archie and Sister Alliece Burns, and also a lady named Mother Blaylock. We traveled to Vernon, Texas, from Frederick, Oklahoma. I did not understand the dream at the time, but I began to share what I had seen. The dream was so vivid that it was as if I had experienced it in person.

I dreamed I was in a home with Mother Blaylock. She was on the telephone calling a family after a death. After we returned to Frederick, Oklahoma, from Vernon, Texas, Mother Blaylock's husband died unexpectedly, and I was at her home making telephone calls to her family. The Lord had allowed me to share the dream with them before it became a reality. I did not completely understand it at the time, but afterward I realized it was a revelation from God.

Revelation 2

My husband had come home from the army and had left driving my car. While he was away, the Lord showed me in a vision that my husband was coming back home, but he would not be in the car. I looked in the mirror while I walked into our bedroom and began to say, "Why is my husband not coming back in the car when he left in the car?" Sure enough, my husband came back home walking, and he was not in the car.

Revelation 3

My husband was still home from the army. His driver's license had expired while he was away, and I had not gotten it renewed. He came to visit me one night while I was in the hospital after surgery. After he left the hospital, the Lord let me know my husband was going to get stopped by the police, but he was not going to get a ticket. Sure enough, he came back to visit and had gotten stopped by the police but did not get a ticket. I told him I already knew it.

Revelation 4

My husband and I were stationed in Fort Leonard Wood, Missouri, and he had gotten paid and left home one night. The Lord let me know he was gambling and had lost money. He came home and I told him, and he said I was a jinx. I knew the Lord had begun to *reveal* Himself to me. My husband also knew something was taking place that did not make him happy. He acted as if I was the cause of him losing money when I was not even there.

The more I would *pray,* the more the Lord would *reveal* Himself to me in dreams or visions. I thank God for entrusting me with His precious gift. I may not be able to convey to some the power of God, but one thing I would like everyone to know that *He is real,* and whatever He spoke in the Bible concerning His Word, He is able to do and He will do. For Jeremiah 1:12 says, "Let us know that God will hasten His word to perform it," through whatever means He chooses because He is the God of the universe, and He changes not.

For I am the Lord, I change not. (Mal. 3:6a)

Chapter 2

Attempted Hindrances

After I had the dream about being in *The Closet of Prayer,* I began to go to St. Mark Church of God in Christ in the morning, shutting myself in and staying in the church to pray. After I prayed alone for one year, I opened the doors of the church with the permission of Bishop Gilkey, allowing others to come in and join me.

After the doors were open for others to come in, the Devil came in also and tried to use a lady to cause confusion and hinder our prayers. One morning as I went in to pray, the lady came in and told me, "Stop that" (meaning to stop praying) and that I was going to have a stroke. I told my son, Tony, about the attempted attack of the Enemy, and he decided to come and join me. The same day an evangelist missionary, Marsha Haney, also came, stating that the Lord woke her up and told her to get up and go to prayer. Soon after she arrived in prayer, the Enemy came in ready to attack, but the Lord did not let the Enemy prevail. When the presence of the Lord would come in, the woman who told me to stop praying would get her things and walk out hurriedly.

On one particular day, the same lady met me in the church parking lot after I had finished praying and stated that the Lord had sent her to help me with prayer. I did not respond in the affirmative. As I left the church parking lot, she followed me,

and as I turned on a street, she turned also. When she saw
that I had reached my destination and the street was a dead-
end street with no outlet, she immediately turned around, as
if she didn't want me to see she was following me, and went
on her way.

Even though I was met with adversities, I wanted to help her
if I could in some way. The Lord gave me the Scripture in Titus
3:10–11: "A man that is an heretic after the first and second
admonition reject; Knowing that he that is such is subverted,
and sinneth, being condemned of himself." I took the Lord at
His word after I shared this with my pastor, Bishop Gilkey,
and he said I may not be the one to help her; therefore I just
continued to pray.

The more you pray and dedicate yourself to the Lord, the
more the Devil will do anything he can to stop the work and
progress of the Lord. As days passed and the prayer continued,
the presence of the Lord would come in the midst in the prayer,
and this individual would get her belongings and rush out of the
sanctuary. One day she just did not show up anymore.

We must always give reverence to God and not man by
staying on the wall of prayer and not letting anything or
anyone deter us. We must do just as Nehemiah, the prophet
of God, did when he heard the wall of Jerusalem was broken
down and the gates were burned with fire. Nehemiah wept
and prayed to God. He consulted with the Lord and rebuilt
the wall. He had not set doors upon the gates when the
adversary (the Devil) sent word to Nehemiah, wanting to
meet with him to do him mischief and cause the work to
cease. Nehemiah sent messengers to his adversary, as it says
in Nehemiah 6:3:

> I am doing a *great* work and I cannot come down:
> why should the work cease whilst I leave it and
> come down to you?

When we are in the closet of prayer, we are doing a *great* work, and we cannot let the Devil cause us to come down and stop the work of the Lord and stoop to his level. The Devil will do anything he can to stop us from praying, praising, or being blessed by the Lord, but with the Lord on our side, we do not have to fear what the Enemy tries to do to us, because the Lord will not let him prevail.

Chapter 3

Definition of Prayer

1. *Prayer is communication with God.* It is the privilege God has granted to every believer to communicate directly with Him.
2. *Prayer is the yearning (desire) of the soul for God.*
3. *Prayer activates (increases) our faith.* The more we pray, the more the Lord reveals Himself to us, and as we see the blessings of God and witness the fulfilling of His promises, our faith is increased.

The Power of Prayer

> For then shalt thou have thy delight in the Almighty, and shall lift up thy face unto God. Thou shalt make thy prayer unto Him, and He shall hear thee. (Job 22:26–27)

The Lord allowed the Enemy to attack Job, who was a perfect and upright man. He was one who hated evil. But Eliphaz, one of Job's friends, had accused him. At one point Job called his friends "miserable comforters." They had vexed him. Job told Eliphaz if he acquainted himself with God (got to know Him) that God would be his defense. So regardless of any circumstance, if we delight in the Almighty and lift up our faces unto God in prayer, He will hear us and be our defense.

Prayer is an attitude of the heart with a sincere utterance in communication with God or the sincere desire and adoration to God. *We have to have pure,* sincere hearts that the Lord is pleased with. We must have surrendered lifestyles that are pleasing to God and that He will accept for our prayers to be answered.

Prayer Is One of the Most Powerful Subjects in the Bible

Prayer sets the atmosphere for blessings (2 Chron. 7:1; Acts 5:15).

> When Solomon had made an end of praying, the fire came down from Heaven and consumed the burnt offering and sacrifices and the Glory of the Lord filled the House. (2 Chron. 7:1)

Prayer changes the atmosphere. Our surroundings are changed and our countenances and speech change. It brings a calm. I like to reach that level in prayer when the prayer is ended and there is a calmness in the atmosphere.

Testimony

A group of SWAT (soul winning around town) team members had finished knocking on doors in the community and witnessing for souls to be won into the kingdom of God. As we were on our way back to our church, we looked ahead of us and noticed a man with his arm around a lady's neck, as if in a choke hold. One arm was around her neck, and an iron rod was in his other hand. He had his hand held back, as if going he was going to hit her. I said to the SWAT team that we should keep walking and praying because in the Bible miracles took place in the shadow of some of the prophets.

> They bought sick in the street, laid them on the bed, maybe the Shadow of Peter when pass by might overshadow them. (Acts 5:15)

We just kept walking and praying, and when we had gotten approximately twenty to twenty-five feet away from the couple, the man dropped the iron rod and they began to walk in an embrace, as if nothing had happened. *Prayer sets the atmosphere for blessings.*

Prayer is the vehicle of communication that help us access heaven. In Acts 12:5–7, Peter was kept in prison and bound with two chains. The church prayed for him without ceasing. When the church begins to pray and gets in one accord, things begin to happen. People can be saved, healed, and delivered.

There is power in oneness. In Genesis 11:1–9 when the children of men decided to build a city and a tower whose top would reach heaven, the people were one, and they had one language. Nothing could restrain them from what they had imagined to do because they were all in one accord. While the church was praying for Peter, the angel of the Lord smote Peter on the side and raised him up, saying, "Rise up quickly." God will avenge His elect (bring satisfaction on our behalf, work for us), for those called by God, who cry day and night unto Him. Nevertheless I tell you He will avenge them speedily. He will work sometimes immediately, as in Luke 18:7–8, but if the Lord doesn't do a work immediately, just keep on praying.

As the church continued to pray for Peter, the chains fell off his hands. The angel told him to gird himself, bind his sandals, cast his garments about him, and follow the angel. In other words, get dressed for your exit to freedom. The things that may have us bound can be loosed and fall off if we are steadfast in prayer. Our minds can be liberated and our souls set free.

When we access heaven with prayer, it serves as a vehicle that can go where we can't go. They could not get Peter him out of jail, but while they were praying, God dispatched an angel and delivered Peter. When we can't be there in person, through prayer the Lord can dispatch an angel for our deliverance.

Testimony

My son Everett went to Las Vegas several years ago and was put in jail. He called me and said, "Mother, they are sending some of the other inmates off to prison from jail." I told him I was going to pray, and within a day or so, he called and stated they came in and said for him to roll them up (in other words prepare for an exit). He came home to Wichita, Kansas, and a date was set for him to return to Las Vegas for a trial to go before the judge. I prayed and wrote a letter to the judge. We heard no more about that case from then until now, and it has been several years. *Therefore prayer is the vehicle of communication that helps us access heaven.*

Prayer is spiritual armor for the saints, serving as a defensive covering or protection.

When the children of Ammon and Moab were coming against Judah, the inhabitants of Jerusalem (God's chosen people) had to fight against them in battle. The Lord said to them in 2 Chronicles 20:17: "Ye shall not need to fight in this battle set yourselves, stand still and see the Salvation [saving or deliverance] of the Lord with you, fear not nor be dismayed [don't be frightened], for the Lord will be with you." The Lord set ambushes against the enemy, and they helped destroy one another.

Not only will the Lord be a defensive covering for you, but He will also bless your offspring. Your entire household and family will be blessed because of your prayers.

Testimony

My grandson's mother had a male friend (who was not my grandson's father) who was not very kind to my grandson. The mother stated that sometimes my grandson would sit in the corner and would not eat. That hurt me to my heart. The mother continued to date the young man even though he was not very nice to my grandson. When my older son, Tony, would take my grandson home after a visit, he did not want to look at his mother's friend. I had to use wisdom because I did not want to make things worse for my grandson after we would leave, especially when I saw a mark on his neck down to the white of his skin that the friend owned up to doing. Someone had him investigated, but they did not find any reason to remove him from the home. The young man thought I was the one who complained and did not want me to come to the home anymore. All I had done was to petition the Lord in prayer, and the Lord had begun to work.

My grandson and his sister told me that once they had seen me outside when I had come for a visit, but he would not let them answer the door. I told the man I was going to tell the Lord on him. I fasted and prayed, and not many days later, there was a complete turnaround. The young man let me come to the home and told me I must have told the Lord. I replied that I did. He later married my grandson's mother and invited me to the wedding. Afterward he seemed to have the utmost respect for me. Regardless of what the problem is, we do not have to fight in any battle because God is our defense. *Prayer* is a spiritual armor for the saints, serving as a defensive covering of protection.

Prayer is the key that channels us to unlock the doors of heaven, giving us spiritual insight and directing us through ways to accomplish the task at hand.

> I will instruct thee and teach you in the way, which thou shalt go: I will guide thee with mine eyes. (Ps. 32:8)

When the children of Israel came out of the land of Egypt, the Lord went in before them by day in a pillar of clouds to lead their way and by night in a pillar of fire to give them light; therefore they had guidance from the Lord to lead them day and night (Ex. 13:21). When you can't see your way, God will lead and guide you every step of the way.

Testimony
Attempted Foreclosure

Several years ago my home was in foreclosure, and the sheriff had even tacked a note on my door. I did not have the money to keep me from losing my home. I prayed and went on a ten-day fast, believing God would work things out.

On approximately the fourth or fifth day of the fast, the Lord spoke to me in prayer and said for me to call a niece of mine who lived in Alaska. I decided to give her a call once I had completed the ten-day fast, as I had set out to do. At the end of the ten-day fast, I gave my niece a call and told her that she had come to me while I was in prayer. She said, "I did?" When I told her that I needed approximately $2,500, she did not exchange words. She said, "Okay," and asked me when I needed the money. Then she stated something to effect that she could have sent it off that day and went on talking about something else.

In the meantime, it came to me at night to get out of bed and pray because my car was going to be repossessed also. I did not get out of bed, but I prayed while I was lying in bed. My son later used my car and drove it to a QuikTrip store, and when he went outside of the store, my car was being towed. I was told that they would sit at the corner of my street and wait until I would leave home to take the car so the neighbors would not see them take it away from my home. My home was in foreclosure and my car was towed away, but after I had fasted and prayed, I knew the Lord could work things out for me. My niece sent me enough money to get my home out of foreclosure and my car back that had been repossessed.

Prior to getting my car back, I was scheduled to go to work, but I did not have any transportation. I had gotten out of bed, and on my way back to bed the Scripture came to me: "I will instruct you in the way which you should go, I will guide you with mine eyes." I climbed back into bed, and *I heard a voice sounded like the bark of a dog saying, "Work, work." I knew that I was going to go to work, but I still did not have a way. Immediately the telephone rang,* and on the other end was a Sister Roshelyn McCoy, who asked, "Sister Gentry, do you need a way to work?"

Therefore prayer is the key that channels us to unlock the doors to heaven, giving us spiritual insight and directing us through ways to accomplish the task at hand.

Prayer is the preparation for danger. It sets miracles in motion.

> He shall cover thee with his feathers and under his wings shalt thou trust. Thou shalt not be afraid for the terror by night, nor for the arrow that flieth by day. For he shall give his angels charge over thee, to keep the in all thy way. (Ps. 91:4–5, 11)

When Saul was after David, the Lord protected him because his mission was not completed. When Daniel was in the den of lions, the Lord locked the jaws of the lions because his mission was not complete.

Testimony

One night while I was in bed, I received a call from one of my daughters, and she seemed to be in a panic, stating, "Mother, if someone comes to the door, don't let them in." Someone had made a threat and said if they could not get to a niece of mine for something she had done that they were not pleased with, I was going to be their next target. They were coming after me. I got out of bed at around two or three in the morning, not knowing the situation or the circumstances, and I began to talk to the Lord in prayer, reminding the Lord of my love for Him, how I lived for Him, and how I did not bother anyone. When I finished talking to the Lord, I went to bed and went to sleep. I never heard or saw anyone. I experienced nothing but peace in my home. The Lord can put an angel of protection all around us, *so prayer* is the preparation for danger.

Chapter 4

Reasons for Prayer

We Pray Because of the Command of God

Pray without ceasing. (1 Thess. 5:17)

Even if we don't feel any immediate results while praying, we must continue to pray because our prayers are going up into the heavenly realm. They are released in the atmosphere and will come up for a memorial before God as with Cornelius in Acts 10:4. They are kept in store for God to act upon at whatever time He sees them as necessary. He may answer them today, next week, next month, or next year, but wait on Him because through our waiting, our souls are blessed.

Sometimes we look for a microwave (quick) fix, and it doesn't materialize. We must keep on waiting because in our waiting, *He stabilizes* us (holds us steady, firm, and steadfast), that we may be able to endure when our trials and tests come.

He maketh my feet like hinds' feet: and setteth me upon high places. (2 Sam. 22:34)

He positions our feet like hinds' feet so we can dig in and climb any mountain that's in our way. In other words, He makes us as surefooted as a deer, enabling us to stand secure. When the problems of this life seem overwhelming, God uses extraordinary means to help overcome strongholds. *He strengthens us*, giving us the power, the drive, and the anointing to accomplish the task that is ahead of us.

He settles us or gives us an anchor we can hold on to. As the storms in this life are raging, we grip onto the solid Rock of Jesus. When we give our problems to God, He will move on our behalf, sometimes when we least expect Him to. God wants us to give every problem to Him and leave them with Him. Cast all your cares upon Him, for He cares for you (1 Peter 5:7). Not only does He just care for us at the moment, but He cares for us always and in every aspect of our lives.

Brethren pray for Us. (1 Thess. 5:25)

Sometimes as we are going through our persecutions, we request the righteous to intercede for us with prayer to help bring comfort and strength. James 5:16 says, "The effectual fervent prayer of a righteous man availeth much." God honors a righteous man or woman's prayers. When you honor God, God honors you.

After Nehemiah honored God in fasting and prayer, he said to the Lord in Nehemiah 1:6, "Let thine ear now be attentive, and thine eyes open, that thou mayest hear the prayer of thy servant." When we pray, Jesus is attentive to our prayer and is sitting on the right hand of the Father interceding (pleading) the case of the righteous. It is just as an attorney in the courtroom pleads the case of his client to the judge and jury, asking for mercy for his client, saying, "Give him another chance. He is remorseful for what he did. He has been faithful in keeping his appointments with the probation officer and has been on good behavior."

Just as the attorney pleads the case in the courtroom to the judge, we have Jesus (the master Attorney) pleading our case to the righteous Judge. He is on the right hand of the Father interceding for the saints (pleading our case), saying, "Lord, they are remorseful for their sins. They are walking upright before You. They are on good behavior. They are good stewards, faithful in attendance to church, faithful in giving their tithes and offerings, and faithful with their talents, Lord, give them another chance." If we want Jesus to plead our case to the righteous Judge, we have to do as Timothy admonished us in 1 Timothy 2:8, "Pray, and lift up holy hands without wrath or doubting."

If we want the blessings God wants to give us, we have to lift up holy hands with our hearts right before God. We must have a heart that is without anger, evil speaking, or malice. If so, when we call upon the Lord, He will hear us and respond favorably to us. Not only do we need to lift up holy hands, but we also need to have faith in God. We must have faith to believe that what He has promised, He is able to perform.

Romans 12:12 says, "Continuing instant in prayer." We have to have a constant spirit of readiness for a right-now prayer (a prayer that is needed when the unexpected happens). We have to have our spirits so in tune with God that we can reach Him in an *instant,* in an emergency, for any problem that could happen at any given moment.

Testimony

On December 25, 2010, I received a call from Oklahoma City, Oklahoma, that a young man, age twenty, was found unconscious at home, rushed to the hospital, and put on life support. The grandmother asked my niece to give me a call and intercede for her grandson. (I had met the grandmother and grandson a few years prior in Memphis, Tennessee, at the holy convocation.)

I began to pray and ask the Lord to spare his life and to give him another chance. On Sunday night, December 26, 2010, I called Oklahoma City, and my niece stated that the young man was now opening his eyes and was breathing on his own. They were worrying if he made it that he could have brain damage. I told her to tell the grandmother to take a telephone into the intensive care unit and put it to the young man's ear. A few minutes later they put the phone to his ear, and I began to pray for the young man, asking him to begin to thank God for his healing even in his spirit.

The next morning, December 27, 2010, I called Oklahoma City again, and my niece stated that the family received a call and was told the young man, J. L., was up walking and talking. Thank God for Jesus and the glory of God being manifested. He made a complete recovery, and I saw him a couple of weeks later in Altus, Oklahoma, approximately one hundred miles away.

Prayer Is God's Chosen Method for Defeating the Devil

Being on Spiritual Watch (alertness)

First Peter 4:7 says, "Be sober [sound mind] and watch unto prayer in order to be aware of the devil." We have to stay alert and not be spiritually asleep in this time of life. As we pray we have to be aware of our surroundings so as not to be caught off guard or succumb to his tricks or overpowered by his devices.

Testimony of Needing to Watch While Praying

Several years ago, after I had completed praying for about an hour after being on my knees in my church, I looked around, and there was a man of another race sitting on steps directly behind me leading up into the pulpit area, watching me. I do not know how long he had been there. I was so engaged in prayer I was not aware of him until I had finished praying. I don't know what he was sitting there for, but that let me know we can't ever lose our focus or let our guard down at any time as a Christian because the Devil is on constant watch, going about seeking whom he may devour or catch off guard. So we have to *watch, as well as pray,* to be aware of the Devil to prevent his attack.

Save the Sinner

> But the Publican, standing afar off would not lift up so much as his eyes into heaven, but smote upon his breast, saying God be merciful unto me a sinner. (Luke 18:13)

We have to humble ourselves with our hearts looking up to heaven, being ashamed of our sins once we acknowledge we are sinners and need salvation. We become godly sorrow from the standpoint that we want to turn away from this world of sin and surrender totally to the Lord. We ask God to come into our hearts as our Lord and Savior, believing that Christ died on the cross and on the third day God the Father raised Him from the dead. He will not only forgive our sins, bringing salvation, but He will also keep us from sin.

Keep One from Sin

> Watch and pray that ye enter not into temptation: the Spirit indeed is willing, but the flesh is weak. (Matt. 26:41)

Prayer helps us keep flesh under subjection. If we don't pray, we will yield to temptation.

> But every man is tempted when he is drawn away
> of his own lust, and enticed. Then when lust hath
> conceived, it bringeth forth sin: and sin, when it
> is finished, bringeth forth death. (James 1:14–15)

Prayer keeps us from yielding to the works of the flesh.

Testimony

In 1984, after I had rededicated my life to the Lord and purchased my own home, a married man I had dated in the past who flew me places, gave me a home, purchased me cars, etc., called me and wanted me to meet him in another city with all expenses paid. I let the man know that I would not come because through prayer the Lord had changed my life. Sometimes when you make a vow to the Lord, the Devil will offer you things you desired to have in the past but were unable to get. He wants to keep you bound, holding you hostage, and making you feel that you need to depend on him for your needs. I am reminded of the Scripture:

> But my God shall supply all your need according
> to his riches in glory by Christ Jesus. (Phil. 4:19)

After I rededicated my life to the Lord, I wrote a letter to his wife and expressed my regret for ever dating her husband since she was aware of the relationship. She said she was glad it was me rather than another young lady she knew who liked him because she felt she would not have wanted him to come back home to her. One year, one of their high school–age daughters ran away from home and came to my home to live. I saw that she attended school and got enough credits to graduate from high school. I then took her back to the city where her parents lived so they could see her march with her former classmates.

When her husband later expired, she had her daughter contact me, but I did not attend the funeral. Therefore *prayer will not only save you but once you are saved, it will keep you from sinning.*

Reveal the Will of God

> Jesus said and I say unto you, *Ask* and it shall be given you, *Seek* and ye shall find; *Knock* and it shall be opened unto you. (Luke 11:9–10)

If we *ask in prayer*, we will know His will. We must ask, not being biased or prejudiced, not choosing what we want, and letting go of what we do not want, giving over totally to His will and wanting what He wants for our lives, for He know what is best for us. We must be submissive to His will.

If we *seek in prayer*, we will find His will. According to His Word, if we seek Him, we shall find Him if we search for Him with our whole hearts. We have to do some seeking and searching *to know and find His will*. We have to have the right motive and have our hearts right before God. The way we search for Him and become in fellowship with Him is by fasting, praying, mediating, and reading his Word.

If we *knock in prayer*, He will open unto us His will. If we open up our hearts and let him in, He will come in and sup with us and we with Him. We can dine with Him. We must open up our hearts and sit at His table, feasting on Psalms and on Proverbs and desiring the sincere milk of the Word so we can grow thereby. Whatever our hearts' desire is when we pray out of a sincere heart, *He will reveal to us His will.*

Testimony

When I purchased my home, I needed $1,000, but I did not have any resources to get the money. I began to talk to God, telling the Lord that He knew why I was by myself because I had a desire to live for Him (and I gave up the things of the world to please Him). I reminded Him of what He said in His Word: *if my ways pleased Him, He would give me the desires of my heart.* Even though the Lord knows all things, I began to talk to God, praying, "Lord, I walk up right before you. I love everybody, and I try to treat everybody right. Lord, I don't know where to go.

I went on to work at Wesley Hospital after talking to the Lord, and that very evening after coming home, I had a beauty appointment scheduled. I told my youngest son, Everett that I had $25 to get my hair done, but I needed $975 more, so I might as well go and get my hair done, and I did.

When I returned home at around seven o'clock from the beautician, my son said, "Mom, some man called." I looked at the number and said to him that I did not know who called, but I would return his call, so I did. When I made the call, the man on the other end of the line stated, "Mrs. Gentry, I will let you have one thousand dollars." I asked him what I needed to do to get it and how soon. He stated, "Tomorrow, and just bring me one check stub and an ID."

When I got off the phone, I called and asked a man I had confidence in if he had heard of anything like this, and he stated he had not. I hung up the phone and said, "If anyone would call me and say they would let me have the exact amount of money I needed and that I talked to the Lord about, it has to be the Lord." *If we ask in prayer, believing, it shall be given.* God is faithful to His Word.

Chapter 5

Qualifications of Prayer

1. *Prayer should be humble.*

And the publican, standing afar off, would not lift up so much as his eyes unto heaven, but smote upon his breast, saying God be merciful to me a sinner. I tell you this man went down to his house justified rather than the other: for every one that exalteth himself shall be abased, and he that humbleth himself shall be exalted. (Luke 18:13–14)

2. *Prayer should be simple.*

But when ye pray, use not vain repetitions, as the heathen do: for they think that they shall be heard for their much speaking. (Matt. 6:7)

3. *Prayer should be sincere.*

The Lord is nigh unto all them that call upon him, to all that call upon him in truth. (Ps. 145:18)

4. Prayer should be done in faith.

But without faith it is impossible to please him: for he that cometh to God must believe that he is, and that he is a rewarder of them that diligently seek him. (Heb. 11:6)

Chapter 6

Positions or Postures of Prayer

When you are in the *closet of prayer*, you have to be in the *right position* (right relationship) with God before your petition can be answered. My pastor, Elder Tony Gentry, made a statement in January 2012 while we were in our Prayer and Fasting Solemn Assembly, saying, "It does not matter what *physical position* we are in when we pray, as long as we are in the *right position of the heart.*" We must have a heart that is connected to God and is dedicated to doing the will of God.

Bowing in Prayer

> And Moses made haste, and *bowed his head* toward
> the earth, and worshipped. (Ex. 34:8)

Moses did not just *bow* with his head toward the earth in this *position*, but he *worshipped* the Lord out of a truthful and a pure heart, with his mind focused on heaven. This is the only worship God will accept. John 4:24 says, "God is a Spirit: and they that worship Him must worship Him in Spirit and in Truth."

Moses bowed his head and worshipped the Lord, and the Lord made a covenant with him.

And he said, Behold I make a covenant: before all the people I will do marvels, such as have not been done in all the earth, nor in any nation: and all the people among which thou art shall see the work of the Lord: for it is a terrible thing that I will do with thee. (Ex. 34:10)

Exodus 34:28 lets us know that Moses was with the Lord forty days and forty nights, and he wrote upon the tablets the words of the covenant (the Ten Commandments). The Lord spoke to Moses and showed Himself mightily because of the right position of his heart as he worshiped Him. The Lord is the same today as He was in the biblical days, and He will still show Himself mightily as He did with Moses if the worship and the position of the heart is connected with Him.

Testimony of Bowing in Prayer

In September 2002 after I began working at Progressive Home Health in Wichita, Kansas, I was in sitting in my office upstairs when I heard a commotion downstairs. I immediately rushed down the stairs, and I saw a lady lying on the floor not responding who had come in for orientation with other nurses around her. I went directly to the lady and *bowed down before her and began to pray.* She began to regain consciousness, and once I saw her beginning to respond, I knew she would be all right. I started to raise her head, but I heard the Spirit of the Lord speak to me and say, "Do not raise her head." I did not want anything to interfere with what the Lord was doing, and as a nurse, and from training I knew that if someone hit his or her head, we are not to move them without a neck support.

Therefore I did not proceed to lift her head, and while *praying,* I said, "Lord, You can allow her to lift up her head," and she began to lift her head without any assistance. The ambulance was called to take her to the hospital. When the ambulance arrived and she was being put on the ambulance stretcher, I prayed again and said, "Lord, You can let her begin talking," and the Lord did just that. I made one more request of the Lord, asking the Lord to let her mind be clear when she arrived at the hospital, and then I went back upstairs to my office. I later asked one of the nurses, Missionary Shirley Patterson, why she did not come and help me pray, and she stated, "Girl, I did not want them to run all of us out of here." *The Lord can answer while you are bowed in prayer.*

Standing in Prayer

> And when ye *stand praying, forgive,* if ye have aught against any: that your Father also which is in heaven may forgive your trespasses. (Mark 11:25)

Testimony of Standing Praying

The Lord gave me that Scripture as I went to pray for a lady who was confined to her home in March 2012. Prior to getting out of my car to go in and pray with her, I opened my Bible to the above Scripture, and as I started ministering to her, I told her I was going to read the portion of Scripture I had opened my Bible to prior to entering her home. I began to read Mark 11:24–26.

> Therefore I say unto you. What things so ever ye desire, when you pray, believe that ye receive them, and ye shall have them. And when ye *stand* praying, forgive, if ye have aught against any: that your Father also which is in heaven may forgive you your trespasses. But if ye do

not forgive, neither will your Father which is in
heaven forgive your trespasses.

After standing, praying, and reading the Scripture to her, she
stated that before I arrived, she was thinking that she needed to
forgive someone she had something against.

I told her the Scripture was a confirmation from God
and shared with her a testimony that a pastor's wife named
Mother Vera Price had shared a few days prior. She said she
had a breathing problem and as a prayer warrior she had prayed
and was not healed, but as soon as she forgave someone she
had something against, the Lord healed her of her condition.
After her testimony she spoke and sang under the anointing
of God in the Kansas Southwest Conference (Spring Workers
Meeting).

The lady I was witnessing to stated that she also had a
breathing problem. I prayed for her, and she stated that her
body was hurting and she had a pounding headache prior to me
praying but the headache had left and her body was not hurting
anymore. It is imperative that we forgive if we want the Lord
to hear our prayers and be forgiven by Him.

Testimony 2 of Standing Praying

On April 21, 2012, while in jurisdictional prayer at New
Philadelphia Church of God in Christ, the Lord spoke to me
as a pain struck me on my head when the glory of the Lord
filled the place that someone must have been healed from a
migraine or very severe headache. Near the end of the service,
I mentioned if anyone had a pain, we would pray. No one
came forward, and then I did what I was supposed to do at
first.

I asked if someone had come in with a headache and the
Lord healed them. A lady named Mother Nettie McClennon

stood up and stated that when she came into the church, her head was killing her, and she kept walking in and out of the church, and then all of a sudden, her head stopped hurting. She further stated that it must have been the Lord who told me that. Then a district missionary, Shirley Hampton, stated that when she arrived at the church, she had a pain in her knee and it was not there anymore. She had left her walking cane that she was using in the back of the church.

Earlier during the same jurisdictional prayer service, I began to minister to the pastor, Elder Richard Scott. I told him that if he stayed on his knees before God, the Lord was going to perform that which had been committed unto him, not the members or his wife or the bishop, but God was going to do it. Later Pastor Scott testified that he had something before the Lord that he wanted done and did not know how he was going to get it done. As I began to minister to him, it became clear to him that the Lord was the one who was going to help him, not the bishop or anyone else but the Lord. The Lord speaks while we are *standing in prayer.*

Lying in Bed in Prayer

> I am weary with my groaning; all the night make
> I my bed to swim; I water my couch with my
> tears. (Ps. 6:6)

Testimony of Lying Down Praying

In September 2011, I spoke to a friend of mine named Mother Maxine Billingsley, and she stated that the church she had been attending had been sold and they were moving. However, she did not want to say where they were going because all of the members of their church did not know. The Lord let me know while I was lying on my bed as I had prayed where they were going, and I told her that it came to me clearly where they were going. She just sort of laughed, letting me know that the place the Lord had given me was the place they had planned to relocate to. The Lord can talk to you while you are *lying in prayer.*

Hands Lifted up in Prayer

> Hear the voice of my supplications, when I cry unto thee, when I lift up my hands toward thy holy oracle. (Ps. 28:2)

Testimony of Hands Lifted in Prayer

At St. Mark Church of God in Christ, for several years I would conduct a prayer and tarry (waiting) service on Friday nights. As we prayed we would sometimes lift up our hands toward heaven while waiting on God to bring salvation and deliverance and to fill the people with the more of His Spirit. The presence of the Lord would come in and bless the people as they lifted up their hands to God while in the closet of prayer. The Lord will bless His people when *our hands are lifted up in prayer.*

On One's Knees in Prayer

> Now when Daniel Knew that the writing was signed, he went into his house; and his window being open in his chamber toward Jerusalem, he kneeled upon his knees three times a day, and prayed, and gave thanks before his God, as he did aforetime. (Dan. 6:19)

Testimony of Kneeling in Prayer

In 2004 I was having problems with my kidneys and was unable to empty my bladder. I was taken to the emergency room, where a urinary catheter attached to a urinary bag was inserted into my bladder for it to drain. I dressed in an extra-long skirt so the bag and catheter would not be noticed and went to the house of God to pray. I was determined not to let this challenge prevent me from communicating with God in prayer. While I was on my knees in the closet of prayer, the Lord let me know that His grace was sufficient for me. Second Corinthians 12:9 says, "My Grace is Sufficient for thee; for my strength is made perfect in weakness." That was all the consolation I needed. I had gone to a specialist who told me I had a blockage. I had problems for approximately a year or two. One day I realized I did not have that problem anymore, for the Lord had healed me. That has been several years now. The Lord yet speaks while we are *on our knees in prayer.*

On One's Face in Prayer

> And he went a little farther and fell on his face, and praying saying, O my Father, if it be possible, let this cup pass from me: nevertheless not as I will, but as thou wilt. (Matt. 26:39)

Testimony of Being Face Down in Prayer

In 2009, after my son had begun pastoring and new members had joined the church, I was lying on the floor in prayer at the church, and I asked the Lord, "How can I help teach the women to better understand the Word of God?" I did not know what to do, but I wanted to be in God's will, so I consulted Him. It came to me to do a book study. This was an effective tool that not only our members benefited from, but others came in and fellowshipped with us during the course of this study, which took approximately two years to complete. The Lord still speaks while on our *faces to God in prayer.*

"It does not matter what position our bodies are in when we pray. As long as our hearts are in the right position with God, then the Lord will hear and answer us."

Chapter 7

Types of Prayer

Prayer of Adoration

> And they worshipped him, and returned to Jerusalem with great joy, And were continually in the temple, praising and blessing God. (Luke 24:52–53)

After Jesus had blessed the disciples and was carried up into heaven, they worshipped Him. In our prayer of adoration, we worship the Lord, letting Him know how much we appreciate Him for who He is, for what He has done, and for what we know He can do and is going to do.

In the closet of prayer, we magnify God and give Him praise, for the Lord is our strong tower, and we can run in and find safety. We let Him know that He is our refuge and strength, a very present help in trouble. Whenever we are in trouble, we do not have to afraid because we know the Lord is our right now help, and whatever we need, we can find it in Him.

Whenever we worship the Lord out of a sincere heart and let Him know how much we love Him, He comes in and showers us with His blessings and His anointing. Then we can call unto Him as in Jeremiah 33:3:

> Call unto me and I will answer thee, and show
> thee great and mighty things which thou knowest
> not.

Testimony of Revelation

Jeremiah 33:3 was revealed to me in such a mighty way as I was working as an IV nurse in a doctor's office. The lab technician had drawn blood from a patient and could not get the test to run on the machine even though she had tried more than once. The Scripture came to me.

> Call unto me and I will answer thee and show
> you great and mighty things which thou knowest
> not. (Jer. 33:3)

I told her to try it one more time, and when she did the test ran right on through without any problems. God still works in *the closet of prayer.*

Prayer of Thanksgiving

> In everything give thanks: for this is the will of
> God in Christ Jesus concerning you. (1 Thess.
> 5:18)

We are to thankful for His blessings, His provisions, His protection, and most of all for His Son, Jesus, who gave His life that we may live. We do not have to use a multiplicity of words when we pray for the Lord to reveal to us His will for our lives.

As we are thankful unto Him and bless His name from a sincere heart, the Lord will speak, for He honors a humble and contrite spirit. Psalm 34:18 says, "The Lord is nigh unto them that are of a broken heart, and saveth such as be of a contrite spirit [a spirit of repentance, sorrow, and humility]." *And He will reveal to us His will.*

Revelation Given While Praying: "Thank You, Jesus, and Yes, Lord"

Bishop J. C. Gilkey Sr., prelate of Kansas Southwest Church of God in Christ, gave a testimony that in 1953, before he accepted the call to preach the gospel, one night after church had dismissed and everyone had gone home, he remained in the church, and there were one or two lights on in the back. He began to pray. He stated that he did not know how to pray, and his prayer for about three hours was, "Thank You, Jesus, and yes, Lord." At around two or three in the morning, while still praying, "Thank You, Jesus, and yes, Lord," the Lord began to speak to him. He opened his eyes and looked at his hands and could not see anything. He stated that it got black and dark, but he kept saying, "Thank You, Jesus, and yes, Lord." While he was praying, a mahogany shield trimmed in gold came down on a gold chain in front of him and stopped. Five directives came up on the shield, with one being repeated:

1. Go preach the gospel,
2. Lo, I am with you always, even unto the end of the world.
3. Be meek and humble.
4. He that believeth shall be saved. He that believeth not shall be damned.
5. Woe unto you if you preach not the gospel.
6. Be meek and humble.

When God finished speaking, the chain pulled the shield back up. He went home speaking in an unknown tongue and praising God. He accepted the call to preach. He said he already knew the Lord wanted him to preach, but he wanted to go back to Friends University first. The next day he looked up the words that were on the mahogany shield and found that they were all scriptural.

Bishop Gilkey further stated that he wrote his pastor a letter and told him the Lord wanted him to preach, and his pastor stated he already knew it. We do not have to use a multiplicity of words for the Lord to hear us. God honors the sincerity of the heart and will *reveal to us His will* as we yield ourselves, being thankful unto Him by saying, "Thank You, Jesus, and yes, Lord," while in the closet of prayer.

Prayer of Confession

> Confess your faults one to another, and pray one
> for another, that ye may be healed. (James 5:16)

Confession of sin opens the line of communication between you and the heavenly Father. King David sinned with another man's wife, committing adultery, and as a result, she became pregnant. To cover up what he had done, he had her husband killed and married her. There was a prophet named Nathan who pointed out to him his wrongdoing in having another man killed. Once David was made aware of his sin, he had a repentant heart and stated that he had sinned against the Lord, as stated in 2 Samuel 12:13. David made a prayer of confession in Psalm 51:2–4.

> Wash me thoroughly from mine iniquity, and
> cleanse me from my sin. For I acknowledge
> my transgressions: and my sin is ever before
> me. Against thee, thee only, have I sinned and
> done this evil in thy sight: that thou mightest be

justified when thou speakest, and be clear when thou judgest.

After David confessed and repented of his sin, the Lord put away (forgave) his sin. When we have a repentant heart, the Lord will forgive us of our sins for His own sake and will not remember our sins (Isa. 43:25b).

Prayer of Supplication

Be careful for nothing; but in everything by prayer and supplication with thanksgiving let your requests be made known unto God. (Phil. 4:6)

Be specific when you pray. Put forth your petitions for those things you need from God in your life. Even though God already knows what we need even before we ask Him, we still are to talk to Him to make our requests known unto Him. John 14:13–14 says, "And whatsoever ye shall ask in my name that will I do that the Father may be glorified in the Son. If ye shall ask anything in my name, I will do." When we ask, we ask in faith, believing that God is going to work on our behalf.

Prayer of Intercession

Prayer of intercession is standing in the gap, with love, being on our knees, and identifying ourselves with the sins of those in prayer. When I intercede for others, I sometime imagine myself or my children in that same position; then I find myself travailing in prayer for that person or persons, pleading on their behalf (standing in the gap).

> And I sought for a man among them, that should
> make up the hedge, and stand in the gap before
> me for the land, that I should not destroy it: but
> I found none. (Ezek. 22:30)

We as saints of God are to stand in the gap and intercede for someone else. Once we have been converted, we are to strengthen our brothers and help bear the infirmities of those who are weak—those who are weak in faith, burdened, and discouraged from the cares and complexities of life. We can travail fervently, consistently, and with an insistent prayer until a breakthrough takes place in their lives.

> Also I heard the voice of the Lord, saying, Whom
> shall I send, and who will go for us? Then said I,
> Here am I; send me. (Isa. 6:8)

Sometimes we may have to make sacrifices to answer the call of God, but the blessings are greater than the sacrifices when we are obedient to God.

Intercessory Prayer Appointment

In 1997 Bishop J. C. Gilkey Sr. appointed me as jurisdictional prayer ministry president for the Kansas Southwest Jurisdiction here in Wichita, Kansas. This ministry is made up of pastors, elders, missionaries, and all members of the forty-plus churches throughout the jurisdiction. The purpose of this ministry is to be a spiritual blessing through *intercessory prayer,* visiting the churches in the jurisdiction as well as leaving a monetary blessing.

Bishop Gilkey was the leader of this ministry before I was appointed. It was an honor to be appointed, but I told him, "I do not know how to pray." He encouraged me by saying, "The

Lord has anointed you to pray." I have never forgotten those words, and they have encouraged me for the sixteen-plus years that I have been over the ministry.

The Lord has strengthened me both spiritually and naturally, allowing us to cover thousands of miles while being in the closet of prayer. Sometimes we would travel four to five hours one way under adverse weather conditions weekly each year. We would pray, minister, eat, and return home. Through this ministry, I witnessed the miraculous power of God. The Lord spoke to Isaiah, saying, "Whom shall I send, and who will go for us?" I said through my obedience to the prayer ministry for sixteen-plus years, "Here am I; send me."

The greatest intercessor was Jesus as He was on the cross for the sins of the world. He prayed, "Father, forgive them, for they know not what they do." He was ridiculed, spat upon, mocked, and beaten, and He suffered and died that we may live. He is now at the right hand of the Father making intercession for the Saints, pleading our cause to the heavenly Father.

We also recognize the power of intercessory prayer when Peter, one of Christ's disciples, was in jail. The church was praying collectively to God without ceasing for Peter. While they were praying, the Lord dispatched an angel where Peter was being held captive, loosed the chains, and delivered Peter out of Prison. Matthew 18:19 says, "If any two of you shall agree on earth as touching anything that they shall ask, it shall be done for them of my Father which is in heaven."

If we come in agreement in prayer, the Lord will dispatch an angel and loose whatever chains are keeping us bound and holding us hostage. The Lord will lose the bondage of discouragement, distress, fear, depression, etc. In Mark 9:23 Jesus said to the father whose son had a dumb spirit and would throw himself in the fire and tear himself, "If thou canst believe. All things are possible to him that believeth." We have to believe God in the impossibilities of man but the possibilities of God.

Other Types of Prayers

1. Prayer of Faith

> Jesus answered and said unto them, Verily I say unto you, If ye have faith, and doubt not ye shall not only do this which is done to the fig tree. But also if ye shall say unto this mountain, Be thou removed, and be thou cast into the sea; it shall be done. (Matt. 21:22)

Thought

Faith can handle whatever problems you are going through. It can take care of the small things in life or the problems that seem huge—that look like they will never leave. Jesus spoke to the problem, and it withered away. We as believers have been empowered by Jesus Christ to speak to our situation, and if we believe God, He will fix it. "There is nothing too hard for our God." Begin speaking to your problem, and by faith you are guaranteed positive results.

2. Prayer of Commitment

> Casting all your care upon him; for he careth for you. (1 Peter 5:7)

Thought

God is willing to take all worries, anxieties, and problems if you bring them to Him in prayer because of His care for you. The song says, "Oh what peace we often forfeit, Oh what needless pains we bear, all because we do not carry everything to God in prayer." God will help and deliver you from any dilemma in your life. God's love and divine care will get you through the best and the worst of times. Trust God to handle your situation.

3. Prayer of Worship

> And they worshipped him, and returned to
> Jerusalem with great joy: And were continually
> in the temple, praising and blessing God. Amen.
> (Luke 24:52–53)

Thought

Our worship should be continuous day and night—"a
never ending praise," always speaking to God with the fruit
of our lips (Heb. 13:15). By Him therefore let us offer the
sacrifice of praise to God continually—that is, the fruit of
our lips, giving thanks to His name. God continues to show
His mercy and lovingkindness every day. The Bible says,
"He commands his lovingkindness in the day time, and in
the night his song shall be with me" (Ps. 42:8). Never stop
praising God because He is faithful to us 365 days a year.

4. Prayer of Agreement

> Verily I say unto you, Whatsoever ye shall bind on
> earth shall be bound in heaven: and whatsoever
> ye shall loose on earth shall be loosed in heaven.
> Again I say unto you, That if two of you shall
> agree on earth as touching anything that they
> shall ask, it shall be done for them of my Father
> which is in heaven. For where two or three are
> gathered together in my name, there am I in the
> midst of them. (Matt. 18:18–20)

Thought

The prayer of agreement by two faith-believing people can
get a reaction from heaven. When the saints get together in
unity and believe God for an answer, God will react. Unity
or corporate prayer is a powerful chain that cannot be broken
when God is in the middle. Let us bind our forces together

to defeat the Enemy during battle in prayer for our families, communities, and nations.

Prayer of Meditation and Quietness

There are times when I hear the Lord speak to me while I am praying. He can also speak to us through meditation and quietness.

> Therefore Eli said unto Samuel, Go, lie down: and it shall be, if he call thee, that thou say, Speak, Lord: for thy servant heareth. (1 Sam. 3:9–10)

So Samuel went and lie down in his place. And the Lord came, stood, and called as at other times, "Samuel, Samuel." Then Samuel answered, "Speak, for thy servant heareth."

I would like to think that if Samuel was lying down to sleep, he was probably still and quiet. The Lord called him four times, and on the fourth time he said to the Lord, "Speak, for thy servant heareth." If we are servants of God, we will listen to God and do those things that are pleasing to Him. Once the Lord gets our attention, He can give us His leading and directions, and we can follow His will.

Once the Lord got Samuel's attention, He gave him directions, and Samuel not only heard the directions but followed the directions the way they were given to him. He listened and followed the directions of the Lord, so in *meditation and quietness* we can say, "Speak, Lord, for Thy servant hears."

Psalm 46:10 says, "Be still, and know that I am God." Sometimes we may not have adequate words to say or know what to do, but at those times, I admonish you not to make a move until you hear from God. Stand still and pray. Rest in the Lord according to Psalm 37: 7a: "Rest in the Lord and wait patiently for him."

We lie down in Him. We walk in Him. We lean on Him. We trust in Him. When we don't know what to say and the words are not adequate enough, we just meditate on His Word, for God knows the thoughts and intents of our hearts. David said in Psalm 139:1–2, "O LORD, thou hast searched me, and known me. Thou knowest my down sitting and mine uprising, thou understandest my thought afar off."

While we rest in the Lord, He can work in us, and our faith will help us believe in the quiet unseen workings of God. Just by resting in His presence we can receive a spiritual transformation by staying before him.

Chapter 8

Lord, Teach Us to Pray

Jesus' disciples could have felt a tremendous lack in their lives as they saw the example of their Lord as He ceased praying in a certain place. In their need one of his disciples said to Him, "Lord, teach us to pray" as John also taught his disciples. Jesus responded to His disciples and also to us in a way that is simple yet so beautiful.

> When ye pray, say, "Our Father which art in heaven, Hallowed be thy name. Thy kingdom come. Thy will be done, in earth, as it is in heaven. Give us this day our daily bread. And forgive us our debts, as we forgive our debtors. And lead us not into temptation, but deliver us from evil: For thine is the kingdom, and the power, and the gory, forever. Amen. (Matt. 6:9–13)

That is what we call the Lord's Prayer. Therefore real prayer is simply a conversation with the "our Father." He used the plural "Our Father." He is your Father, my Father, and Jesus' Father.

Today we as followers of the Lord sense our need to learn how to pray. We can knock on doors, talk on the telephone, and invite people to our prayer groups, only to find out that when we meet together, "We do not know how to pray as we ought," so we ask the Lord to teach us to pray.

Develop a Spirit of Prayer

1. Be Disciplined

We must be disciplined, using training that enforces us to be obedient to the will of God through prayer. If we are unable to keep the designated time, we must be disciplined and committed enough to pray in such a way as to not let anything or anyone stand in our way of daily communicating with God.

2. Develop a Habit

It is helpful to develop a time of prayer, which will help us to be more disciplined, but if we do not have a designated time to pray, we should develop a *habit* of praying—of listening and talking to God—to get to know more about Him and what it take to please Him. The more we communicate with one another, the more we get to know more about that person. We recognize the person's likes and dislikes. We understand what it takes to satisfy him or her. It is the same way with God. The more we consult Him and talk to Him, the more we get to know Him and what it takes to please Him.

We want to get to know the Lord, the power of His resurrection, and the fellowship of His suffering, being made conformable unto His death. In as much as He suffered in the flesh, we have to arm (prepare) ourselves likewise, realizing we too must suffer. After Christ went through suffering, being ridiculed, talked about, spit upon, and beaten and died for our sins, He got up out of the grave with all power in His hand, and if we want to be conformable unto His death, we too much suffer. The more we enter into the *closet of prayer,* communing with God out of a sincere heart, the more we will get to know Him.

We may enter into the *closet of prayer* at different times, just as long as we are consistent in coming before the throne of grace.

> Let us therefore come boldly unto the throne of
> grace, that we may obtain mercy, and find grace
> to help in time of need. (Heb. 4:16)

We do this so we may obtain mercy (blessings, compassion, and favor of God) and grace (that unmerited divine assistance given to us by God for our regeneration and sanctification) as we develop a habit of prayer.

Praying In One Accord

> These all continued with one accord in prayer
> and supplication, with the women, and Mary the
> Mother of Jesus, and with His brethren. (Acts
> 1:14)

Jesus gave a command to His apostles, whom He had chosen, letting them know that they should not depart from Jerusalem until they received the baptism of the Holy Ghost, and once they received the Holy Ghost, He would give them power to witness at home and abroad. After Jesus finished teaching the people concerning the Holy Ghost, He was taken up in a cloud into heaven. After the apostles saw Jesus' ascension into heaven, they followed His command, went into an upper room, and joined some of Jesus' disciples and women. They were all gathered together with *one accord in one place.* They were praying, waiting to be filled with the baptism of the Holy Ghost.

They had one directive in mind, having the same focus as they petitioned the Father. While they were praying in one accord, the Holy Ghost fell upon each of them. When we are united in prayer, miracles happen; *bodies are healed, Salvation takes place, and those who are bound are set free.*

Chapter 9

Different Times of Prayer:
Morning, Noon, Evening, and Night

Morning

> And in the morning rising up a great while before
> day, he went out and departed in a solitary place
> and prayed. (Mark 1:35)

He needed a place to be alone—a place to communicate
with the Father while everyone else who was close to Him
was asleep. Sometimes we may need to get by ourselves and
get alone with God, without any interruptions or any possible
interruptions, shutting out all distractions and letting the Lord
minister to us as we petition Him in prayer.

Testimony While Praying in the Morning

Early one *morning* before day, the Lord visited me in a
disturbing dream, letting me know that my son Everett who
lived in Las Vegas, Nevada, had a problem and had gone to
the hospital. I got out of bed, went into my family room, and
prayed, shutting out all distractions. After I had prayed, the Lord

gave me peace, letting me know that my son was going to be all right. I was able to go back to bed and go to sleep. I told my oldest son, Tony Gentry, about the dream. The next day Everett called and stated that he had gone to the hospital but that he was all right. *The Lord can meet us early in the morning.*

Noon

Evening, and morning, and at *noon*, will I pray, and cry aloud: and he shall hear my voice. (Ps. 55:17)

David said, "Evening and morning and *noon [three times a day]* will I pray."

As for me, I will call upon God; and thy Lord shall save me. (Ps. 55:16)

There is no guessing in the word *shall*. David knew from personal experience that the Lord would save him and protect him from the hands of the Enemy or his so-called friends.

He said in Psalm 55:12 that the one who came up against him was not an enemy; if so he could have borne it. He said, "Neither was it he that hated me that magnified himself against me; then would I have hid myself from him: but it was thou, a man my equal [someone just like me]."

He said, "My guide [one who advised me and gave me counsel] and mine acquaintance [one that I knew]. We took sweet council together [enjoyed one another, were happy with each other]. And walked into the house of God in company [went to church together] but wickedness was in their dwellings on the inside." Wickedness was in their hearts. Therefore David said, "I will call upon God, and he shall save me [deliver and keep me]. So three times a day I will pray," one of the times being *noon*.

Testimony While Praying at Noon

While at *noon* prayer at St. Mark Church of God in Christ on Twenty-First and Maplewood in Wichita, Kansas, I was compelled to tell the person who was praying to the far right of me that the Lord was going to bless her. I did not know who it was until after I had prayed, and then I told her what had been given to me. It was a lady named Sister Marsha Ector-Haney, who sang in the choir at that time. She later became an aspiring missionary, married, and an evangelist missionary, and afterward the Lord elevated her to state evangelist elect lady. *So the Lord will meet and speak to his people at the noon hour.*

Evening

David not only prayed morning and at noon but also in the *evening, as in Psalm 55:17. Evening,* morning, and noon ... When King Saul was after David to kill him because of jealousy, he not only prayed in the morning and noon, but he also prayed in the evening (three times a day). He knew where his help came from, so he said in Psalm 121:1–2, "I will lift up mine unto the hills from whence cometh my help. My help cometh from the Lord, which made the heaven and the earth." Psalm 119:164 says, "Seven times a day do I praise thee." David not only prayed, but he also gave God praise.

David went on to say in Psalm 34:1–2a, "I will bless the Lord at all times: His praise shall continually be in my mouth. My soul shall make her boast in the Lord." I too am going to bless the Lord at all times. Every day will I bless the Lord and give Him the glory that is due in His name. I will bless Him in the good times and in the not-so-good times, for I know He will help me, for I have chosen His precepts. Psalm 119:173 says, "Let thine hand help me; for I have chosen thy precepts." Once we choose the precepts of God, walking in His ways and obeying His commandments, the Lord will hear us and help us.

Testimony While Praying in the Evening

My grandson Artis DePaul Kelly would go to prayer with me at St. Mark Church of God in Christ when he was about seven or eight years old. As I would be on my knees in prayer, he would lean over and lay on my back. When my son began pastoring in 2008 and I would go to prayer, he continued to go with me. One day he went to the piano and began to play a tune. After listening to him, I began to sing and realized he was putting some of the keys together.

On April 7, 2011, on a Thursday *evening,* I turned and prayed for my grandson's hands, and after praying for his hands, and with my eyes closed, I could hear a melodious sound, as if someone was playing skillfully on the organ. When I opened my eyes, there was no one in the church playing.

I asked DePaul within the next couple of days what he thought it meant when I had prayed for his hands and thought I heard someone played on the organ. He stated that it meant God was going to bless him to play the piano and the organ.

The Lord has given him a special gift and a listening ear to be able to hear a song and begin playing it. He also can pick some of the strings on the guitar with song. When asked how he is able to do that, he states, "I don't know." His gift has not been perfected at this time, but I know God can do exceedingly abundantly above all we can ask or think according to the power that works in us, even *when we pray in the evening.*

Midnight

> And at *midnight* Paul and Silas prayed and sang praises unto God: and the prisoners heard them. And suddenly there was a great earthquake so that the foundation of the prison were shaken: and immediately all the doors were opened and everyone's bands were loosed. (Acts 16:25)

Once the keeper of the prison awoke and saw the prison doors were opened, he pulled out his sword and would have killed himself, thinking the prisoners had fled. Paul spoke up and said, "Don't do any harm to yourself, for we are all here." The keeper fell down before Paul and Silas and said, "Sirs, what must I do to be saved?" And they said, "Believe on the Lord Jesus Christ and thou shalt be saved and thy house."

Testimony While Praying at Midnight

For several years before the convening of the Kansas Southwest Jurisdiction Conventions, which is held in March and July, I would coordinate a prayer shut-in at the Kansas Southwest Headquarters at St. Mark Church of God in Christ. At *midnight* we would have an anointing service. During one prayer shut-in at *midnight* the Holy Ghost fell, and a Sister Carla Hoy, who was professing salvation but not the baptism of the Holy Ghost, began to speak in an unknown tongue as the spirit gave utterance. The Lord baptized her in the Holy Ghost, according to Acts 2:4: "And they were all filled with the Holy Ghost and spake with other tongues." *God will work and speak at midnight.*

Night

> And it came to pass in those days, that he went
> out into a mountain to pray, and continued all
> *night* in prayer to God. (Luke 6:12)

If Jesus went out from the people into a mountain to pray,
that let me know that there is a blessing in stealing away in a
solitary place and talking to the Lord, without distractions or
interruptions. We can do a reassessment of our lives and ask the
Lord to give us the directions He wants us to take for ourselves.

> Trust in the Lord with all thine heart and lean not
> unto thine own understanding. In all thy ways
> acknowledge him, and he shall direct thy paths.
> (Prov. 3:5–6)

As long as we pray and stay in the *closet of prayer,* the Lord's ears
will be attentive to the prayer made to Him. Second Chronicles
7:15 says He will direct us and keep us on His divine path
as long as we consult Him in all our ways. When we awake
each morning, we should consult Him for directions. As we go
throughout the day and into the *night,* we should acknowledge
the Lord, asking Him for directions, and He will give us the
answer we need and direct our path.

Testimony While Praying in the Night

My sister, Missionary Annette Archie Rhodes, stated she
had shut herself in her church for three days, praying. While
shut in day and *night,* the Lord spoke to her and told her to
tell her husband that they should take out insurance on him,
which would include paying off the house, two vans, and
the car upon his death. After the shut-in, they enrolled in an
insurance that would be in effect twenty-four months after the

date they had applied for it. Eighteen months after her husband, Superintendent Lathan Archie had taken out the policy, he passed away. The Insurance Company wrote her a letter and denied paying the claim. She told her daughter, Sister Chiffon Ingram, "Let's pray again," knowing what the Lord had told her to do while in prayer day and *night.*

They prayed again, and Sister Ingram stated that the Lord showed her in a dream that the people were sitting at a conference table, and they were writing a check. Within a matter of days they paid off the house, two vans, and the car and sent Missionary Archie-Rhodes a check for her personal use. The Lord saw the sacrifice made day and night, honored the request, and directed her path.

Personal Times Spent in Prayer and Fasting

- For years I would pray for at least one hour to two hours daily.
- Sometimes I stayed in prayer from 9:00 a.m. to around 3:00 p.m. at my church, asking for help from the Lord.
- In 2006 till 2008, I fasted 174 days out of two years as well as prayed.
- One year I fasted for three days every other week for one year.
- I would fast seven, ten, twenty-one, thirty to forty days up to a certain period of time during the day, as well as praying.
- I would fast for long periods of time because I wanted the Lord to do something for me, with me, and through me. I knew the greater the sacrifice, the greater the blessing. I was willing to make the sacrifice to receive the blessing.

Chapter 10

Hindrances to Prayer

1. Known Sin

> If I regard iniquity (Sin) in my heart, the Lord
> will not hear me. (Ps. 66:18)

If there is known sin of any type in our hearts, the Lord
will not hear us, for the Lord's ears are open unto the righteous;
therefore, if I regard iniquity in my heart (hold onto it, keep,
or cherish sin in my heart), the Lord will not even listen to me,
but if I have a heart of repentance, the Lord will hear me.

If we have sin dwelling on the inside and want to get rid of
it, all we have to do is ask the Lord to forgive us as David did
in Psalm 51:9: "Hide thy face from my sins, and blot out [erase,
do away with] all mine iniquities."

Talk to the Lord and ask Him if there is any sin of omission
(something I may have omitted doing, that you wanted me to
do, or should have done and didn't do), blot it out. If there is
any sin that I have committed, blot it out, (take it away, erase
it). We must ask for forgiveness for our secret sins, the sins no
one is aware of but us. Psalm 51:4 says, "Against thee, thee only,
have I sinned, and done this evil in thy sight." The sight of God
is what counts because "the eyes of the Lord are in every place,
beholding the evil and the good" (Prov. 15:3).

Testimony of Forgiveness

My niece Naomi, who lived in Oklahoma City, was expiring from cancer. I went to visit her. She knew that someone had stated that she was going to be healed, but she told me it seemed so far away. I knew the Lord did not tell me that, for I had seen her in the casket in a dream (someone who looked just like her mother and she did).

She asked me what she needed to do if she had wronged someone (*known sin*). I told her to ask them to forgive her, and if she could not get in touch with them, just ask the Lord to forgive her. She then responded in the affirmative.

Two weeks later the Lord called her home. Before the Lord called her home, my sister, Mrs. Virginia Burns (her mother), stated that she said to her, "The Lord loves me. Stop praying for me. I see a light brighter than any that I have ever seen, and I want to go to that light." She went on and expired.

She did not want any *known sin* to be a hindrance when she went before the Lord. Prior to visiting my niece, I had planned to go and visit her in two weeks after the date I went. My son Everett said to me, "Mother, go now." I took his advice and followed the leading of the Lord through him. I was able to go and minister to my niece. It is important to listen to what a person has to say, for there is a reason for every conversation.

2. Insincerity: Not Serious, Just Going Through the Motions

> And when thou prayest thou shalt not be as the hypocrites are: for they love to pray standing in the synagogues and at the corners of the streets, that they may be seen of men. Verily I say unto you, they have their reward. (Matt. 6:5)

Once we realize our sin, if we pray or conduct our lives as hypocrites (profess one thing and live another), *insincerity* does not benefit anyone, not even ourselves. It does not uplift, rebuild, restore, or renew. When we pray, we pray to the Father in heaven, and He and He alone can and will reward us.

So when we pray, we pray to our Father, the Creator of the universe, and the maker of everything in it, including us. We pray to our Father who art in in heaven. He looks down on us and sees our every move. He knows our every thought and cares about our every need. Hallowed (holy) is His name. His name is holy, and His ways are holy. If we are holy, we pray as holy to a holy God. He said in 1 Peter 1:16, "Be ye Holy in all manner of conversation of conversation."

3. Unbelief—Doubting, Lack of Confidence Will Hinder Our Prayers

> But let him ask in faith, nothing wavering. For he that wavereth is like a wave of the sea driven with the wind and tossed. For let not that man think that he shall receive anything of the lord. A double minded man is unstable in all his ways. (James 1:6–8)

When we see the wave of the sea, we do not know which direction it may take from one time to another. It may go one direction one time and another the next time. It is unstable. That is the way we are when we doubt. We are unstable and waver. James said, "For let not that man think that he shall receive anything of the Lord."

A double-minded man is unstable in all his ways. There are two thoughts going through the mind. One thought is that the Lord will fix the situation, and the other thought is, *I don't know if He will or not.* If we doubt God with uncertainty, we need to ask the Lord to increase our faith, as the disciples did in Luke

17:5. We must ask the Lord to make our faith greater so we can believe His Word unconditionally, without doubt.

> Therefore I say unto you, what things so ever ye desire, when you pray, believe that ye receive them, and ye shall have them. (Mark 11:24)

The way we receive faith is through the Word of God, by seeing the miracles, hearing the testimonies of others, and not forgetting what the Lord has done for us.

Romans 10:17 says, "So then Faith cometh by hearing and hearing by the word of God." We believe God through faith. As we read the Word of God and witness the miracles done by faith in the Word of God, then our faith will increase. We then can have that confidence in Him, without doubting, because *doubt* will hinder our prayers.

4. Requests Not in God's Will

> And this is the Confidence that we have in Him, that, if we ask anything *according to His will*, He heareth us: And if we know that he hear us, whatsoever we ask, we know that we have the petitions that we desired of him. (1 John 5:14–15)

Prayer Hindered If Not in God's Will

After David had an affair with Bathsheba (who was a married woman), she became pregnant with his child, and he tried to cover it up by having her husband (Uriah) come in from battle to lay with her. Uriah refused to go in to his wife and be intimate with her, and therefore the child could not be passed off as his. After Uriah was intimate with his wife, David had Uriah put in the forefront of the hottest battle so he could be killed.

After Uriah's death David married Bathsheba, who delivered a son who David loved. But since David had committed a sin against God, He sent a message to David letting him know the child would not live. The child became very sick, and David fasted and prayed for his son to live. He even lay all night upon the ground, but the child died anyway. After the child died, David got up, washed his face, ate, and went on in the ways of the Lord. *It was not in God's will for the child to live.*

Testimony of Not in God's Will

On June 16, 2006, I received word that my grandson who had been a 4.0 student and never had been in any major trouble before was arrested for being involved in a murder. I did not know of anyone in my immediate or extended family who had been charged with murder, and he was a child who did not cause trouble. (He was a child who the Lord showed me through prophecy that my son was going to father, even to the brightness of his eyes.) On March 26, 2005 (on my birthday), he came to visit, and the Lord led me to talk to him for approximately one or two hours concerning school, friends, and the Lord. I also talked to him about making right choices, so as not to get into any trouble. I had prayer with him, and he left.

Prior to the murder charge, I had a dream that I was with a group of ladies from the church, and there were some relatively small snakes bothering them. I spoke and said, "If you do not bother those snakes, they will not bother you," but as soon as I entered the church, a humongous snake came at me with great force. I could feel him around me, but he didn't touch me.

I asked, "Where is he?" I knew he was close to me, but he couldn't seem to get to me. I later told my son Tony about the dream, and I said, "Whatever this is going to be, it is going to be something big." I told him to check on my grandson. My youngest son, Everett (his father), was out of state at the time. My question was, "Is something going to happen to my grandson?"

Approximately two weeks prior to the murder, I decided to go on a three-day fast each week for four weeks, and the fourth week I was going to go on a three-day fast for my grandson. I had fasted two weeks of the four-week fast. I fasted on June 6, 7, and 8 and June 13, 14, and 15. I did not make it to the fourth-week fast before the murder took place.

After that I fasted for 174 days from 2006 till 2008, with prayer included, until the day of his sentencing, asking the Lord to have mercy on him and not allow him to do prison time, but if he did do time, for him not to do an extended period of time.

The day of his sentencing was November 13, 2008. I went to prayer, as I normally did, at St. Mark Church of God in Christ prior to the verdict. I testified that if the Lord did not allow him to be acquitted, I was going to do as David did when he fasted and prayed for his child to live after he had become very ill. The Lord did not grant his wish, and the child died. Therefore after the death of his child, he got up and ate and continued in the ways of the Lord (2 Sam. 12:15–23).

My grandson was found guilty on November 14, 2008, and sentenced to twenty-five years with a chance of parole after the twenty-five years. I do not believe he will be there that long, and neither does he. There were two other men involved, and they were found guilty with no chance of parole. After the sentencing I continued in the ways of the Lord, remaining in *the closet of prayer.*

It was not in God's will for him to be acquitted, even though *I had fasted and prayed for 174 days from June 25, 2006, to November 2008, but it was not in God's will.* From the first time I received the news of him being involved in a murder up until now, the Lord has given me peace. I was fasting and praying prior to the incident for something else, but the Lord prepared me for what was ahead. Romans 8:28 says, "And we know that All things work together for good to them that love God, to them who are the called according to his purpose."

It was prophesied to me by a Pastor Herman Hicks that the Lord was going to use him there in prison, and that prophecy has come to pass. My grandson has now finished religious courses. He has been teaching other inmates and has found favor with the prison officials, as well as other inmates. During a seven-day prison revival, several religious leaders were asked to come in and speak for six of the seven days of the revival, and he was the only one from the prison population chosen to speak and represent the inmates on the seventh day.

In November 2013, my grandson stated to me that he is there for a purpose and that God is working things out. He is not anxious, not stressed, and not worried about anything, and this is just a transformation. He never imagined this would be the avenue God would use for him, but this was necessary. It is amazing how something we consider a tragedy can turn out to be a blessing. He is learning and realizing that this is not just for him, but the Lord is using him to help others grow and see their purpose. It has been a blessing to him as he has been a blessing to someone else. He states *"he is learning and doing things he has always wanted to do in a place he has never wanted to be."* He said it makes him think of Joseph in the Bible and how the Lord used him to help others. He also stated that once while he was on his knees praying, he began to speak in an unknown tongue. The Lord filled him with the gift of the Holy Ghost. *God works according to His will.*

Praying in God's Will

The Lord sent Isaiah to Hezekiah to tell him to get his house in order, "For thou shalt die and not live." *Hezekiah turned his face to the wall and prayed unto the Lord,* reminding the Lord of how he had walked before Him with a perfect heart and had done that which was good in His sight. The Lord told Isaiah to go and tell Hezekiah, "I have heard thy prayer, I have seen thy tears: behold, I will add unto thy days fifteen years." Read Isaiah 38:1–5.

Testimony of God's Deliverance

In September 1965, while living in Frederick, Oklahoma, after the delivery of my first child (Pastor Tony Untra Gentry), I went into unconsciousness for three days, and the physician did not know if I would live or die. My family was called to my bedside, including my mother, who came from Arkansas to be at my bedside. The Red Cross was contacted and was instrumental in getting my husband home from the army.

Once during those three days I came out of unconsciousness momentarily, and I could see all the people around my bed. *I could not speak*, but I thought to myself, *When I go out this time, I am not coming back anymore.* I later drifted back into unconsciousness, and the God of all mercy and grace bought me back. I had a praying mother and father. James 5:15 says, "The prayer of faith shall save the sick, and the Lord shall raise him up: and if he have committed sins, they shall be forgiven him." Our prayers will be answered if we pray in God's will.

Another Hindrance to Our Prayers

5. Refusal or Being Unwilling to Forgive

> And when ye stand praying, forgive, if ye have aught against any: that your Father also which is in heaven may forgive you, your trespasses [sin]. But if ye do not forgive neither will your Father which is in heaven forgive your trespasses. (Mark 11:25–26)

Forgiveness is a requirement for the saint, and if we really love the Lord, we will love the Lord's people, and it will be easy to forgive. We will want what is best for them as we want the Lord to do what is best for us.

My bishop, Bishop J. C. Gilkey, said the Lord will not hold you responsible for what someone else do to you or how we are treated, but He will hold us responsible as to the way we react to the treatment. God is a fair and just God. If God is fair and if we are like Him, we too must be fair and just. It cannot be one sided. Micah 6:8 says, "He hath shown thee O man, what is good, and what doth the Lord require of thee, but to do justly, and to love mercy, and to walk humbly with thy God."

God has showed us what is *good* by being an example. He showed what He *requires* by His actions. We have to be *just* in our dealings with one another (impartial). *Love mercy.* We must be kind one to another and walk *humbly* with our God. We should love mercy to the effect that the same mercy we want for ourselves we must show to others.

> Therefore if thou bring thy gift to the altar, and there rememberest that thy brother hath aught against thee; Leave there thy gift before the altar, and go thy way; first be reconciled to thy brother, and then come and offer thy gift. (Matt. 5:23–24)

When we are praying, offering up our problems to the Lord, and while in prayer we remember that someone has something against us or if we have something against someone else, we are to stop praying and go and be reconciled with our brother. Go and ask for forgiveness and make things right between you and your brother (or sister), and then come again to the Father and offer to Him again the problem we presented before for things to be right between yourself and God.

Forgiveness clears the atmosphere for blessings from the Lord, brings wholeness to the body, and clears the mind so it is ready to receive from the Lord. If offenses come between your brother and sister, repent and repent quickly

I am glad that *the Lord put a spirit of forgiveness in me* that compels me ask for forgiveness whether I have wronged others or not. Even if I feel they have any hard feelings toward me and I do not have any toward them, I have no choice but to go and ask for forgiveness so I can have peace and move forward in the Lord. Even if you are not treated kindly and others try to do things to hinder you or your progress in the Lord, go to those who have offended you. Do not talk against them. Continue to be loyal to them and work with them if they allow you to do so. We have to believe the Word of God, which says in 1 Corinthians 10:13:

> There had no temptation taken you but such as is common to man: but God is faithful, who will not suffer you be tempted above that ye are able; but will with the temptation also make a way to escape, that you may be able to bear it.

We must realize that the Devil can't touch us unless the Lord allows it to happen.

Some people may be planted in your life to help bring you to your purpose and keep you on your knees. As long as we trust the Lord to do what is best for us, we can say as Joseph said when his biological brothers turned against him. Genesis 50:20 says, "But as for you, ye thought evil against me; but God meant it unto good, to bring to pass, as it is this day to save much people alive."

Once I go to an individual and ask for forgiveness, I get a release in my spirit, knowing I have done what the Lord requires to move forward to my destiny. I want to receive all the rewards and benefits the Lord has for me in this present life, but most of all I do not want any hindrances when I bow before the Almighty in that great judgment day.

So if we feel our brothers or sisters have anything against us, even if we don't have anything against them, we are to go to them and be reconciled with our brother or sister, and then our heavenly Father will receive our request. *Refusing to forgive can hinder our prayer life.*

Chapter 11

Seasons in the Closet

The Physical and Spiritual Closet

We have natural seasons of spring, summer, fall, and winter determined by the variations in temperature and climate on the earth for physical purposes. Seasons dictate to us how we dress, what activities we engage in, what we eat, our moods, and our attitudes. There are also spiritual seasons Christians go through for a divine purpose. "To everything there is a season, and a time to every purpose under the heaven" (Eccles. 3:1).

A natural closet is a place of storage. It's a place where you can store your clothing or certain items to be left until the time needed, to be retrieved and worn in any season. *The closet of prayer* is a place where we store up prayers in heaven. We place our prayers in spiritual reserve (they are bottled up in heaven) to be used for any situation, whether immediate or a later time appointed, for whatever season we experience in our lives. It is a place of refuge and solace.

> The name of the Lord is a strong tower, the righteous runneth into it, and is safe. (Prov. 18:10)

The name of the Lord represents the Lord Himself, His presence, and His power. He alone is a strong tower in whom men may find true security. Run in and find deliverance, run in and find peace, run in and find salvation, run in and find healing, and run in and find shelter from the storm.

Men may seek other means and things to fortify themselves, but when the shattering realities of life come, it is going to take the honor and favor of the Lord, which can be found *in the closet of prayer,* to provide lasting security.

In the natural closet, you have clothing for the seasons of spring, summer, fall, and winter. At the appropriate time or season, we can retrieve what we need for the occasion. It is the same way in the *closet of prayer;* we store up prayers in heaven for any occasion needed or any situation we may encounter, no matter what season we are in our lives.

> And the smoke of the incense, which came with
> the prayers of the saints, ascended up before God
> out of the angel's hand. (Rev. 8:4)

Season of Spring—March, April, and May

In the natural closet in the season of spring, a raincoat and rain gear are placed in the closet to be used for spring showers. It is a time when seed has been placed in the ground or soil and is being fertilized and cultivated. The rain begins to fall, flowers begin to bloom, and grass begins to grow. It is the breading season  for butterflies. A new birth or new beginnings take place as the seed is resurrected, and a new transformation takes place. It reflects a springing up of plants, and new life begins.

In the Closet of Prayer in the Spring

In the spiritual closet, salvation (new birth) takes place. New ministries are birthed, and new opportunities are given.

> I am crucified with Christ, nevertheless I live, yet not I but Christ liveth in me and the life I now live in the Flesh, I live by the faith of the son of God who loved me and gave His life for me. (Gal. 2:20)

> Therefore if any man be in Christ, he is a new creature: old things are passed away; behold, all things are become new. (2 Cor. 5:17)

We see things differently and think differently because we are different. This old sinful nature that was in me in the flesh has been killed and has been replaced with a new birth (the Spirit of Christ). Resurrection has taken place. Christ was resurrected (rose) from the grave, and I was resurrected from a sinner to a saint), when I received the new birth of Jesus Christ, then salvation began in me. We experience the newness of life—a life in Christ Jesus.

We have pulled off the old man with his deeds and have put on the new man, which is renewed in knowledge after the image of Him who created him, according to third chapter of Colossians. Putting on as the elect of God, holy and beloved, bowels of mercies, kindness, humbleness of mind, meekness, longsuffering, charity, forbearing one another, and forgiving one another, which can only come about by being in *the closet of prayer.*

As we put on the new man as the elect of God, we have been selected, chosen, and adopted into this royal family, being made in the image of God, not as the physical man but now as a spiritual man. We act like God, talk like God, and are examples of His righteousness because we are the righteous of God. We do not conform to this world but have been transformed (changed, made new) by the renewing of our minds.

We then have begun a new life in Christ. "A place to begin a new life" is the motto of our church, the Emmanuel Church of God in Christ, in Wichita, Kansas, where my son, Pastor Tony Untra Gentry, began to pastor in 2009.

Therefore in *the springtime, new birth, new opportunities, and new ministries are manifested.*

Prophecy in Ministry

One Saturday doing the early years of the Kansas Southwest Prayer Ministry that was organized in 1996 while I was visiting his church in Arkansas City, Kansas, Superintendent James Watson called me another Mother Elsie Shaw. Mother Shaw was an international prayer leader who the Lord used in prayer and prophecy.

Prophecy of Intercessor

In February of 2009, a national evangelist came to Wichita, Kansas, and conducted a revival at the St. Mark Church of God in Christ and prophesied to me, stating:

1. Your latter years will be greater than your beginning.
2. Great woman of God, I call you a woman of God because you are a great intercessor.
3. You intercede when people are asleep, and as a great intercessor, you pray all the time. Some people may *say* they pray all the time.
4. God has given you a special gift of interceding. God shows you the condition of the people.

5. I will go as far as to say I sense the angelic presence of God. I smelled the savor of flavor in your house.
6. God is going to do some awesome things for you.
7. Know I have been in your house.
8. God said you know how to get to my heart.
9. You are going to wave your hands, and people will be healed and delivered.
10. You will walk by, and people will be delivered.
11. God said He has gifted you with His angelic presence.

Divine Revelation of Ministry

On June 15, 2008, a lady by the name of Sister Moore came to me and stated that she had a dream about me, and in the dream I was in a meeting with a large crowd. She could see people and wheelchairs. She stated that she felt it was going to be something big.

Prophecy of Outreach

On June 10, 2009, Mother Bernice Tucker stated to me while I was a member of St. Mark Church of God in Christ that I was *going to reach millions.* She said, "The Lord may have to move you from here for the people to know who you are. People are going to be calling you, maybe for a week of prayer revival at a time. People are going to give you money." She further stated, "You could use some money." I just made a note and pondered this in my heart.

Prophecy of Blessings

On Wednesday, May 19, 2010, Superintendent Mark L. Gilkey said to me in a Kansas Southwest Church District

Meeting, "God is going to bless you because you stay there praying. The people have not seen how *the Lord is going to bless you.*" I continue to do as Mary, the mother of Jesus, did in Luke 2:19: "But Mary kept all these things, and pondered them in her heart." Therefore I am pondering these things in my heart. Superintendent Gilkey stated to me again on January 1, 2014 that he appreciated my prayer life and that the Lord is going to work through me mightily. I have begun to see the manifestation of the power of God.

On Sunday, August 8, 2010, Apostle Lathan Archie stated to me while in prayer during our family reunion that I was going to begin to pray out of myself into heaven, and the Lord would reveal Himself to me, and people would give me money. The Lord was going to give me new dimensions of prayer, not levels. We call it prophets. The Bible calls it seers. He further stated, "You are going to see things in the Spirit and prophesy in prayer."

I claim that prophecy because *in the closet of prayer* some of those things have begun to take place.

Testimony of Breaking of Strongholds

The Lord saved my brother-in-law, Brother O. J. McElroy, who came to my parents' home and was inebriated. A chair was set out in the living room, and my brother-in-law sat in the chair. Because of the power of prayer and the Lord using my sister, Missionary Annette Archie, the Lord saved him and delivered him from alcohol. He remained saved until his demise.

Prophecy of Salvation

One night as I was sleeping, I dreamed one of Bishop Gilkey's daughters stated for me to read 2 Chronicles 6:9 in regard to my son Everett. When I awoke out of the dream, I opened the

Bible to 2 Chronicles 6:9, which says, "Notwithstanding thou shalt not build the house; but thy son which shall come forth out of thy loins, he shall build the house for thy name."

My son has not accepted the Lord as his personal Savior, but I have unwavering faith that the Lord is going to save my son. I believe it so much, that once my son left home and did not return during the night, and someone had gotten killed on the same night. After doing some checking, the legal authorities told me my son had gotten killed and asked if I needed someone to come with me to the morgue to identify him. I said no, that I could come alone. I sat down at my dining room table and said that I believed he was saved before he died because I stand on the promises of God. As I was sitting, trying to decide what type of suit I would bury my son in before I went to identify him, I received a call from the sheriff, and he stated that the person who was killed was not my son. Therefore, regardless of the circumstances I have the confidence that the Lord is going to save him.

> He staggered not at the promise of God through unbelief; but was strong in faith, giving glory to God. And being fully persuaded that, what he had promised, he was able also to perform. (Rom. 4:20–21)

Prophecy of Elevation to Bishop

Prior to Elder J. C. Gilkey Sr. becoming Bishop J. C. Gilkey Sr., I went to him and told him that I saw him go up in a dream. In other words, he was being elevated to a higher position in the church. He said that maybe he went up to heaven. I said, "No, I saw you move up in the church." He later was appointed as the Kansas Southwest Jurisdiction bishop of the Church of God in Christ, one of the highest offices of the church.

Prophecy of Breaking Ground

Prior to Supt. J. C. Gilkey Jr. starting his church, I went to him while he was still a member of his father's church and told him I had dreamed that he was leaving. In the dream he was breaking ground. He smiled and told me he was leaving and for me not to tell anyone, not even his parents, because they did not know. I told him I would not. He stated that he was planning to leave in order to start his own church. A few years later during his pastor and wife's appreciation service, I asked him if I could tell the prophecy, and he said I could. He has been pastoring for several years at present.

Prophecy of Elevation In Ministry

Every fifth Sunday of each month; for approximately fifteen years I was appointed by my pastor, Bishop J. C. Gilkey Sr., to conduct the services. These services were for the purpose of giving honor and recognition to the pastor's wife. Before each service I would try and go on a three-day fast. One day while I was conducting the Sunday-morning service, as soon as I sat down, *the Lord let me know my daughter-n-law, Missionary Carlotta, was going to be appointed over the fifth-Sunday service.* When I told her that, she said, "Oh no, Mother!" Sure enough, the bishop consulted her about being over the fifth-Sunday service for the following year, when the new appointments were to be made, but he did not want her to mention the upcoming appointment at that time. She said that she stated to him, "Mother already knows." I know the Lord to be a revealer.

Revelation to Obey God

On Friday, August 26, 2011, my brother-in-law, Rev. Hogan, spoke to me by telephone, reminding me that my sister,

Missionary Annette Archie-Rhodes, is gone (deceased). This sister he was referring to was used by the Lord in a mighty way in praying, prophesying, and winning souls for Christ. He went on to say that it was for me to take her place, further saying for me to do what the Lord wanted me to do.

My sister and I would travel to several holy conventions, from state to state, and I saw how the Lord would use her in miraculous ways. Elisha asked Elijah for a double portion of his anointing in 2 Kings 2:9–10:

> And it came to pass, when they were gone over, that Elijah asked Elisha, Ask what I shall do for thee, before I be taken away from thee. And Elisha said, I pray thee, let a double portion of thy spirit be upon me. And he said, thou hast ask a hard thing: nevertheless, if thou see me when I am taken from thee, it shall be so unto thee; but if not, it shall not be so.

When my sister expired, I was there in the room when she transitioned from earth to receive her everlasting reward.

Revelation of God's Extended Hand

On Friday, July 8, 2011, after I had prayed on the national prayer time line for the needs of the people, Pastor Martin begin to pray and minister to me. He stated, *"I see the Lord ministering to you, Mother Gentry,* for your hands are full. God said I am meeting your needs as you meet other's needs. You minister through prayer to so many, and God said, 'I am extending my hands toward thee. I have not forgotten your labor of love.' So God speak into her, remind her that she has begun a good work. He has begun a good work in you, Mother Gentry and has not forgotten your labor of love and said he is going to complete it."

> For God is not unrighteous to forget your work,
> and labour of love, which you have shown toward
> his name, in that ye have ministered to the saints,
> and do minister. (Heb. 6:10)

In February 2013 I listened to Pastor Edward Martin pray on the prayer time line. He was doing a corporate prayer, but I listened with an open heart. In his prayer he said that the Lord see that ministry, and he heard the Holy Ghost say that He sees your gift when nobody else recognizes it, and He is going to do something about it. He went on to say, "The Lord sees you, and He is going to bless you."

I realize that whatever purpose the Lord has for our lives, He is going to perform it; therefore we must stay on our knees in the closet of prayer.

> No good thing will He will withhold from them
> who walk upright. (Ps. 84:11)

Season of Summer—June, July, and August

In the natural closet in the summer season, lightweight clothing is placed in the closet for warmer days. It is the longest season of the year. We witness sunny days, flowers are in full bloom, and things around us look brighter. It's a time of laughter and joy. We are in the summer of our lives and go on what we have learned in the spring.

In the Closet of Prayer in the Summer

In the spiritual closet, spiritual development takes place. It's a time when we can learn to study Scripture better. We can reap the benefits of the seed we planted in the spring to receive a bountiful crop. The seed has to be cultivated with prayer to develop spiritually, and our lives can possess the fruit as in Galatians 5:22.

The Fruit of Love

Love is a self-denying, self-sacrificing action word with Christlike characteristics. Love is not partial and is not just for a select few but for everyone. With Christlike characteristics we can love the unlovable and those who despitefully misuse us and say all manner of evil against us. We can treat them as brothers. The love of God constrains us to do right. There is no evil in love. Love wants to do well, and if I should find myself not wanting to do the right thing toward anyone, then I know I must be lacking in love. *In the closet of prayer,* love can be rekindled, nourished, and healed.

Testimony of Love

When I found my husband being unfaithful with another woman and he bought her to our home and told her to come in, she was afraid because she did not know what I might do. My husband then told her if she did not come in he would hit her in the head. Because of the love God had placed in my heart I could not let him hit her in the head, so I told her to come in and I would not bother her. She came in, and I talked to her as a mother. He later had children by her, and when we talked about rekindling our marriage, he asked me how I would treat the children. I told him I would treat them as if they were my own. *In the closet of prayer,* the Lord can let you love unconditionally even in adverse situations.

The Fruit of Joy

Joy means to delight in and experience pleasure. We can hear and experience joy and gladness. Psalm 51:8 says, "Make me to hear joy and gladness; that the bones which thou hast broken may rejoice." When everyone around us is despondent and sad and we believe the Lord with all our hearts, we can have joy unspeakable and full of glory. First Peter 1:8b says, "Though now ye see him not, yet believing, ye rejoice with joy unspeakable and full of glory" because the joy of the Lord is our strength.

This joy that is down on the inside you can't convey to anyone like you feel it. It is unspeakable, yet it is full of the glory of God. The more we pray, the more the Lord gives us His joy. It is not temporary but everlasting, and it is something nobody can give but the Lord. Isaiah 59:19 says, "So shall they fear the name of the Lord from the west, and his glory from the rising of the sun. When the enemy comes in like a flood, the spirit of the Lord will lift up a standard against him." There is joy in the closet of prayer.

Testimony of Joy

I was in church one day and was called out of the church by one of the members who stated she wanted to see me. As soon as I got out of the sanctuary to greet the person, she started to ridicule me. I did not understand the reason for the ridicule and tried to explain to her that I liked her and always complimented her, and her response was, "Yes, but you did not mean it." I was taken by surprise and had no idea she felt that way. I thought she really liked me. When she finished telling me what she had to say, she walked off and left me standing there.

When I went back into the sanctuary, I felt the presence of the Lord come on me, and I shouted victoriously. The Spirit of the Lord will come upon us and overpower us and cause us to lift up a standard against the enemy, giving us liberty.

I continued to love the person and would help her if needed in any way possible.

Testimony 2 of Joy

> And it shall come to pass that before they call, I will answer; and while they are yet speaking, I will hear. (Isa. 65:24)

I went to prayer one morning at St. Mark Church of God in Christ knowing that I needed some extra money. I said to the Lord, *while in prayer,* that I would possibly place a call to a place I had worked at previously and see if they would give me a few hours of employment. When I arrived home from prayer, without placing the call, I looked at the telephone and had received a call from that agency offering me a job. God can work before we call, and while we are yet speaking, He will hear and give us *joy* unspeakable and full of His glory. *There is joy in the closet of prayer.*

The Fruit of Peace

Peace is the tranquility of the soul. This is the peace that is given by God, as spoken of in Isaiah 26:3: "That will keep us in perfect peace, when we keep our minds stayed on Him, because we trust in Him." When we get up each morning with our minds focused on the Lord and thanking Him for a new day, we can have peace. When we go throughout the day, thanking God for His provisions, we can have peace. As we prepare to recline for the night, thanking God for making it through the day and asking Him to take us through the night, we can have peace. As we continue to meditate on the greatness and goodness of God, we can have great peace. Psalm 119:165 says, "Great peace have they which love thy law: and nothing shall offend them." There is *peace in the closet of prayer.*

Testimony of Peace

On April 14, 2012, when it was announced that a tornado was moving toward Wichita, Kansas, and it could be disastrous, with the loss of lives, the Lord gave me peace. They announced for everyone to take cover immediately. My son Pastor Gentry and his wife were in Fort Worth, Texas, visiting at the time. We spoke on the telephone, and I told him the greatest cover we could have was the protection of Jesus. I will not tempt God, but I trust Him with my life. The tornado did hit Wichita, Kansas, and did an estimated $283 million worth of damage, with no loss of lives. I thank God for His hand of protection over so many of our homes and our families. *There is peace in the closet of prayer.*

The Fruit of Long-Suffering

Long-suffering is patiently enduring and enduring injury, even when it's difficult. As the Lord is long-suffering with us, we should be long-suffering with one another. Second Peter 3:9 says, "The Lord is not slack concerning His promise, as some call slackness; but is longsuffering to us-ward, not willing that any should perish, but that all should come to repentance." The Lord is not slack or slow but is patient. He is giving us a chance to repent and turn from our unsaved ways and follow Him so we can escape the punishment of hell.

> I therefore, the prisoner of the Lord, beseech you that ye walk worthy of the vocation wherewith ye are called, With all lowliness and meekness, with *longsuffering,* forbearing one another in love. (Eph. 4:1–2)

> Thou therefore endure hardness as a good soldier of Jesus Christ. (2 Tim. 2:3)

Testimony of Long-Suffering

In this spiritual walk, I have experienced challenges and misunderstandings and been lied about, persecuted, ignored, misused, and abused—*but God* has sustained me and kept me from the hands of the Enemy as I have stayed *in the closet of prayer.* I am reminded of the words of the late Presiding Bishop J. O. Patterson, when he said, "I have been a strong man in this church." I can say I have had to be a strong woman in this church. Even when being mistreated, I would not retaliate. I have gone and asked for forgiveness even when I had done no wrong, even when others did not reciprocate. Bishop Gilkey used to tell us as his members that the Lord will not hold us responsible for the way someone treats us, but He will hold us responsible for the way we treat the person.

On November 14, 2008, I dreamed that there was a large snake that would just lay and watch me, and it could cause a lot of damage. I wanted to know if others could see the snake. Once I shared with the late Mother Willie Pearl Houston when I would see something, telling her that it looked like everyone could see what I was seeing. She responded to me, "Everyone don't see that."

We as saints cannot share with everyone the things the Lord reveals to us. We are to love and try to protect one another in order not to have others looking at them in a bad light. My mother used to say, "I would rather suffer wrong than to do wrong," and I have tried to govern myself in the same way. My son preached a message once titled, *"Thank God for the Experience."* Therefore I thank God for the experience, knowing that the Lord will not allow the Enemy to harm His people without His permission.

> The Lord is on my side, I will not fear. What can man do unto me? (Ps. 118:6)

In the closet of prayer, the Lord let the Scripture be real to me, as in Jeremiah 12:5:

> If thou hast run with the footmen, and they have wearied thee, then how canst thou contend with horses? And if in the land of peace wherein thou trustest, they wearied thee, then how wilt thou do in the swelling of Jordan?

There is *long-suffering in the closet of prayer.*

The Fruit of Gentleness

Gentleness is sensitivity of disposition and kindness of behavior founded on strength and prompted by love. Gentleness evidences itself in a willingness to yield. Paul behaved toward the Thessalonians in a gentle manner, stating to them that he could have been burdensome, as the apostles of Christ. He showed them affection, stating that they were dear to him.

> But we were gentle among you, even as a nurse cherisheth her children. So being affectionately

desirous of you, we were willing to have imparted unto, not the gospel only, but also our souls, because ye were dear unto us. (1 Thess. 2:7–8)

Christ cultivates the qualities of *gentleness in the closet of prayer.*

Testimony of Gentleness

When I worked at Wesley Medical Center in Wichita, Kansas, there was a lady who was very unkind to me. She would talk to me in unpleasant ways, and I remained gentle toward her. I went to her and asked her to forgive me if I had harmed her in any way. She seemed to accept the apology, but as soon as we would get around the other nurses, she would start being unkind again. I went to her friend and told her I had gone to her and asked her for forgiveness, but she still did not treat me nice. Her friend stated to me that she did not like anyone she thought could do anything better than she could. When we were helping patients and if she could not perform a treatment and I could, she would not ask me.

I would go sometimes and eat alone and cry and tell the Lord, "You said You would fix it." I tried to be gentle and did all I knew to do, yet she did not seem to care for me.

I continued to talk to the Lord about the situation. One day this nurse and I were on call together (we would be called to different floors of the hospital to do treatments). On this particular day we were passing through the lobby area on one of the patient floors, and it came on the TV that someone had gotten killed in Wichita. I tried to be gentle, holding a conversation with her and stating that the incident on TV could be us. That day she asked me do a treatment she was unable to do, in putting a tube into a child's stomach. I thought maybe things were going to turn around. I had prayed day after day.

I went to work the following day, and as I walked into the lounge area where the nurses were gathered, I was told that a nurse who was in her forties or fifties had gotten killed in an accident that night. I felt that the Lord would fix the situation. I'm not saying that the death occurred because of me, but David said:

> He suffered no man to do them wrong yea, he reproved kings for their sakes; Saying touch not mine anointed, and do thy prophets no harm. (Ps. 105:14–15)

Testimony 2 of Gentleness

There was another nurse who would be very hateful to me and would just frown as I would talk to her. Sometime she and the lady in the first testimony who got killed would seem to team up in being unkind to me. One day I was trying to make conversation with her as we were riding in an elevator, and I said, "Maybe you would be able to work where I am working if I was no longer working there," and she seemed to frown. Approximately one to two weeks later, I went to work and was told that this nurse, who was about thirty-five years of age, was sitting up in her chair, and the Lord called her home. We can show *gentleness after being in the closet of prayer.*

Testimony 3 of Gentleness

In 1987 I worked in a physician's office doing IV therapy treatments. My father became ill with cancer, and I went out of state to Arkansas to be with him. While I was away, there was a patient who wanted to start treatments who was told I was out of town. I remained with my father for approximately one week until after he expired. When I returned back to

Wichita to do the IV therapy on the patient, the lady was very upset that I was not there to do the treatment earlier. I tried to explain to her in an apologetic, gentle way that I had no control over death and that my father had expired. Regardless of the explanation, she was still not happy. I went to work one day soon after that and was told the lady was found dead in the bathroom.

Testimony 4 of Gentleness

After I had worked at the hospital in Frederick, Oklahoma, for a few years, I was appointed as the director of nurses of the nursing home. After I was appointed, one of the licensed nurses decided to leave and go and work at one of the plants. I bought her into my office and talked to her and tried to get her to stay, but she refused. Sometime later the Lord allowed a tornado to come through the city, and her home was one of the ones that was destroyed.

The Fruit of Goodness

Goodness is of a high quality or standard on an absolute scale or in relation to another or others. It is described as being along with righteousness and truth. The Christian life in its truth is likeness to God, and as God is good to us, every chance we get we should do good to someone else. Galatians 6:10 says, "As we have therefore opportunity, let us do good to all men, especially unto them who are of the house of faith." Psalm 33:5 says, "He loveth righteousness and judgment: the earth is full of the goodness of the Lord." Goodness is love in action. There is *goodness in the closet of prayer.*

Testimony of Goodness

One day I needed some money, and I went to a place called Children's Fashion Exchange, which is a place where you could take children's clothing and exchange it for other clothing or sell it. I needed money for household expenses until I received my next paycheck. As soon as I returned home with the money, there was a knock on the door, and I opened the door to a grandmother who was left to take care of her grandchildren because one parent had been put in jail, and the other parent I believe was using drugs, and she needed money to help with the children.

I gave her all the money I had just gotten for myself, and I went in the freezer and gave her almost all the food I had in the freezer. I knew the Lord would take care of me. Therefore *goodness* or *love* constrains us to give. Let's remember the words of David in Psalm 37:25 "I have been young, and now am old; yet have I not seen the righteous forsaken, nor His seed begging bread." I knew the Lord would take care of me. The Lord provided for me then until I got paid and has provided for me ever since. Up until now, God has been good to me. There is *goodness in the closet of prayer.*

The Fruit of Faith

> Now faith is the substance of things hoped for,
> the evidence of things not seen. (Heb. 11:1)

Faith is evidence in the spiritual realm. It is not a blind acceptance but a spiritual substance. The more we read God's Word and pray, the more our faith will increase. Romans 10:17 says, "So then faith cometh by hearing, and hearing by the word of God." As we are readers of the Word, digest the Word, meditate on the Word, and are doers of the Word, our faith will increase.

If we are lacking in faith, we can ask the Lord as the disciples did in Luke 17:5: "And the apostles said unto the Lord, Increase our faith." The disciples felt their faith needed to be increased; therefore they petitioned God. If we want our faith to increase we too need to petition God, continue to read His Word, and remain *in the closet of prayer.*

Testimony of Faith

> Therefore I say unto you, what things so ever ye desire, when ye pray, believe that ye receive them and ye shall have them. (Mark 11:24)

In the middle part of the 1990s, I had told Missionary Mary Gouldsby, one of the members who would ride with me to church and prayer, that I was going to purchase a Cadillac. A few months later I took my son with me to a Bulgers Cadillac dealer in Wichita, Kansas, and saw the car I wanted to buy, but I was told I did not qualify for it. I told them I would be back to purchase the car. I took the serial number of the car and left.

We would drive through the car lot from time to time, and the car was still there. One day my son and I drove through the lot and noticed the car was no longer there. A few weeks passed, and the car still was not there. I told my son that when I got ready to purchase the car, it would be there.

Approximately two or three months had passed total, and on the day I got ready to purchase the car, we went back to the car lot and told them the type of car I was looking for. They said they just gotten one in that was on the inside that had been sold, but the buyers were unable to keep it, so they bought it back. I told my son, "I bet that's my car," and sure enough, when we saw the car, it was the same one. The price had been increased, but once I showed them the serial number and the original listed price a few months prior, they honored it, and I left in the Cadillac. *There is faith in the closet of prayer.* If we believe and do not doubt, the Lord will bring to pass whatsoever we desire when we pray.

Testimony 2 of Faith

In 2010, I owned a 2000 Cadillac, and in March of 2010, the car dealer said I needed a new engine for the car, which would cost $7,000. I did not have $7,000 for an engine. The car looked good on the outside. The upholstery was nice and it drove smooth, but it had an internal problem. Sometimes we look good on the outside, but we have an internal problem. I am reminded of the Scripture in 1 Samuel 16:7b: "For the Lord seeth not as man seeth; for man looketh on the outward appearance but the Lord looketh on the heart."

I kept adding oil and coolant, but it would run out. I said I was going to continue to drive the car until it stopped completely or the Lord felt it was necessary for me to get another one. I knew with an engine problem I would not get much for it if I traded it in.

I kept trusting God and going to my church, where I would open up the doors and get into *the closet of prayer.* In the last few weeks that I drove the car to prayer, the Lord kept dropping in my spirit that I was going to have an accident in the car and it would be totaled, and I would get another one. I would say, "Lord, I am not going to do anything of my own to cause an accident because my grandson, Elias, may be in the car, and he may get hurt." Therefore I would drive exceptionally slow. I continued to go to prayer, and the same thought would come to me day after day.

On March 15, 2010, when I was not thinking about an accident after leaving the state conference spring workers' meeting for Kansas South Jurisdiction, I had an accident. The car was totaled. My grandson was in the car, but neither of us was hurt. The insurance company paid me the total amount for the car that I would have received if it did not need an engine.

We as saints know that all things work together for the good of those who love the Lord, and whatever God does, He does it well, because Proverbs 10:22 says, "The blessing of the Lord, it maketh rich, and he addeth no sorrow with it." So if God allowed an accident, there will be no sorrow with it, and we will receive a blessing.

I told the Lord the type of car I wanted—the year and color, including the interior. A missionary, Mother Joan Vann, said for me to tell the Lord what I wanted and He would give it to me because He could trust me. That was a confirmation of what I had already done. I came home from church on a Sunday night after I had purchased a newspaper and in the paper only one car was listed that fit the exact description of the 2006 Cadillac CTS, pearl, with a beige interior, that I had said that I had wanted. I felt in my spirit that was my car.

When I went to the car dealer to purchase the car, they asked me what type of job I had, and I said I did not have a job. They began to negotiate with the bank for me, telling them I could get a job anywhere being a nurse. They let me drive away with the car before the loan was approved. After I drove the car for approximately ten days, I received a call from the car dealer and was told they had found someone to carry the loan for a considerable amount less than they had told me when I drove the car off the lot.

God is true to His word. "Don't stop praying, the Lord is nigh, don't stop praying, He will hear your cry. The Lord has promised and His word is true, don't stop praying, He will answer you."

Meekness in the Closet of Prayer

Meekness is a calm temper of mind, not easily provoked, a submission to God and unselfishness to our fellow man. Meekness allows us to walk humbly before the Lord.

> He hath shown thee, O man, what is good; and what doth the Lord require of thee, but to do justly, and to love mercy, and to walk humbly with thy God? (Micah 6:8)

Testimony of Meekness

After my son became my pastor, it was a humbling experience as mother/member, but I had to be submissive to him as my leader in a spirit of meekness, realizing that my son watched over the most important part of me, and that is my soul. I am glad and blessed to have him as my pastor. He is a man God has called to do a work for Him. My son was a loyal, dedicated, and devoted servant to our pastor, Bishop J. C. Gilkey, Sr., for approximately thirty years. He would go into the Church after Bishop Gilkey would leave and lay before God in prayer. Once he became pastor, he would spend hours in the church in prayer, petitioning God for the people of God.

I am reminded of the Scripture in Micah 6:8: "He was shown what was good, and what the Lord required of him in trying to do justly, love mercy, and walk humbly with our God." As a servant of God, I have tried to walk humbly before Him. With my son as pastor, the mother-son relationship took backstage, and I do my best by praying in the church and for the church, trying to help him fulfill the Great Commission of winning souls and to keep him and the members encouraged. It is necessary to have a spirit of meekness to be submissive to the will of God and carry out the wishes of God and my son as pastor.

Temperance in the Closet of Prayer

Temperance is moderation in action, restraint. We will maintain a balance and self-control in our lives as we walk in the ways of the Lord. When we possess the fruit of the Spirit, against such there is no law. There is not a natural law or a spiritual law that is against the characteristics of the fruit of the Spirit, and *temperance* is one of them. We will have it if we have Christ in our lives.

Testimony of Temperance and Prophecy

There was a lovely missionary who loved me and my family and would spend countless hours in my home. I loved her and her family also, but my love extended to all men, and I never wanted to put myself in a place or be too familiar with anyone where I would not be clear whether I heard from God or the person. There were times when I would tell her to go home because she had a family, and I did not want her to spend long hours away from them. Once when I mentioned to her that I did not want to keep her away from her family, her response was she had it all together, and I told her, "But I want you to keep it together."

She was dear to me and to my family. I went to sleep one night, and the Lord showed me in a dream that this person was getting too close. In the dream there was a small alligator-type creature that had gotten so close that I could feel the warm breath of the creature on my body, and the Lord spoke to me in the dream and said, "Move over." When I woke up, I had moved my body over. Before I woke up out of the dream, the Lord gave me a Scripture. I woke up, opened my Bible, and began to read the Scripture He had given me.

Masters; give unto your servants that which is just
and equal; knowing that ye also have a Master in
heaven. Continue in prayer and watch in the same
with thanksgiving. Withal praying also for us that
God would open unto us a door of utterance,
to speak the mystery of Christ, for which I am
also in bonds. That I may it manifest as I ought
to speak. Walk in wisdom toward them that are
without, redeeming the time. Let your speech
be always with grace, seasoned with salt, that ye
may know how ye ought to answer every man.
(Col. 4:1–6)

God will give directions in every aspect of our lives when we pray.

In the Season of Fall—September, October, and November

In the natural closet in the
fall, you will find a light jacket
and a little warmer clothing for
chilly days. The *transition* from
summer into winter is when
the nights become noticeable
earlier. It is a time when we can
see the evidence of our work
and a time to see where we have
come from and where we need

to go. It is a colorful time of year. *Leaves are falling off.* That
is the way of *protecting* the trees for when the winter months
come.

If the leaves remain on the trees, water will escape as water
vapor through the tiny pores in the leaves. This way the tree

can conserve energy and stay alive. It is a time to *reassess* what directions we will take when winter comes. It's a season where the colorful trees are the *transition* of summer into fall, having both the abundance and the limitation of our everyday lives. Many changes occur during the fall months.

In the Closet of Prayer in the Fall—Habits Fall Off

In the closet of prayer in the fall, there is a cutting away and pruning to get rid of the old man (old sinful nature) and put on the new man, which after God is created in righteousness and true holiness (Eph. 4:24. *We are loosed from strongholds*— the things that have a tight grip on us, holding us back, and preventing us from fulfilling the purpose the Lord has for us. *It is a time to rid ourselves of the weights that are hindering our progress with the Lord. It's a time of overcoming obstacles, stresses, distresses, and complexities that have us bogged down in order to restore, protect, and deliver us from the hand of the Enemy.* We then can be prepared to go through the gloomy days of our lives where the days look dark and suffering takes place to be able to weather the storm in the winter.

It's a time when God is doing something in our lives, even when we don't see it. It's the gap between today and tomorrow. It's a time God is preparing us for the last season in our lives—the season of old age, which is not the end of life but full of the harvest of good things.

When we want to overcome obstacles and rid ourselves of unwanted habits, we need to increase our prayer life and add fasting with the prayers. When I decided I wanted the Lord to do something special in my life, I decided to stay longer in *the closet of prayer.* I would go to church at St. Mark Church of God in Christ on Friday nights and *pray for four hours, from 8:00 p.m. till 12:00 a.m.*

Fasting with Prayer in the Closet

Fasting is abstaining from water and food for the purpose of focusing on God for wisdom and direction. It's a spiritual discipline that helps us crucify our fleshy desires to connect more with God for a spiritual and physical *transformation*. It invokes the hand of God to revoke the hand of the Enemy. Fasting helps us get rid of weights, habits, and strongholds. It destroys yokes, looses the ones who are bound, and sets the ones who are oppressed free.

> Is not this the fast that I have chosen? To loose the bands of wickedness, to undo the heavy burdens, and to let the oppressed go free, and that ye break every yoke. (Isa. 58:6)

If we have *strongholds (habits, unwanted attachments)* that are hard to get rid of and we have prayed and prayed, and still have not gotten relief, we need to add fasting with our prayers. In Mark 9 Jesus' disciples were unable to cast the deaf and dumb spirit out of a young man who would tear himself, foam, gnash with his teeth, and pine away. The disciples asked Jesus, "Why could not we cast him out?" Jesus answered them by saying in Mark 9:29: "This kind can come forth, by nothing but prayer and fasting."

Testimony of Fasting

One year I fasted every other week for three days and nights for the entire year. When I came off the fast, Bishop J. C. Gilkey, Sr. (my pastor at the time) talked to me in the entrance of the church about seeing a little cloud about the size of a man's hand, saying there was *a sound of an abundance of rain,* as in 1 Kings 18: 41, 44 as Elijah, "the prophet of God," spoke to Ahab, telling him to "get up, eat and drink; for there is a sound of abundance of rain, telling him to Prepare his chariot, and get thee down, that the rain stop thee not." Elijah prophesied to Ahab, telling him to prepare himself and that there was an abundance of rain even though he did not see the rain with his natural eyes, but he saw it through the eyes of faith.

The more we fast and pray, the more our faith will increase, and we will experience an abundance of rain and "the miraculous works of God." *Yokes will be broken, bodies healed, and protection, transition, restoration, deliverances, etc., will take place.*

Guidance through Prophecy

I would go and pray on Friday nights for four hours nonstop at St. Mark Church from 8:00 p.m. till 12:00 a.m. On this particular night I entered the church doors, along with my two daughters, Michelle, and Marchelle (Marci), as well as Missionary Mary Gouldsby and Mother Joann Vann.

I began to prophesy what the Lord was giving me. I said, "Girls, when this man comes into the church, do not go to the door alone, but go together." In my spirit a man was coming into the church unannounced who was not a member. I continued to proceed into the church to pray. In the meantime Mother Vann said to my daughters, "Your mother must be tired," not knowing that the Lord was speaking through me. As I proceeded into the sanctuary, the Lord let me know that the girls would not know what to tell the man when he came in. There needed to be someone in the back of the sanctuary, but I did not express that to anyone.

In the meantime Mother Vann did what the Lord had put into my spirit. I looked up and noticed her seated in the back of the sanctuary. Each time someone would enter the sanctuary, I would look up from praying and would notice the girls going to the door together. The next time I looked up, I saw Mother Vann coming down the aisle of the sanctuary with the man the Lord had showed me. He may have come in with a wrong motive, but as we prayed for him, Mother Vann, stated he almost fell out under the anointing power of God. I got back on my knees and asked the Lord to give me a word. I randomly opened my Bible to Isaiah 58:11, where the Word of the Lord said, "And the Lord shall guide thee continually." I was asked if I knew someone was coming in the church; I told them no. This further confirms that *the Lord is a revealer in the closet of prayer.*

Protection through Prophecy

When my son, Pastor Tony Gentry, was a teenager working at Burger King in Wichita, Kansas, I took him to work to open the store early one morning. After I let him out of the car, *the Lord let me know that something was wrong. I did not see anything out of the ordinary, but I kept looking back to see if I could see anything.* I knew if I called the police I would not know what to tell them. I continued to go home and just began to *pray.* After I was home for approximately one or two hours, I received a call from my son telling me that when he entered the Burger King, there was a burglar in the store. The person had removed the safe from its original location, and it was in the middle of the floor. My son stated he ran out the back door of the store to go to another business to call 911 and came face-to-face with the man outside. He looked at him and continued on his way. The Lord did not allow him to be harmed. *There is protection in the closet of prayer.*

Prophecy of Removal

In 2001 or soon after Mother Maxine Billingsley was appointed as state supervisor of the Women's Department of Kansas Southwest Jurisdiction, I dreamed she resigned from office. I told my son, Pastor Tony Gentry, and also my sister in Kansas City, Missouri, Mother Chrystell Draper, and she reminded me that she had not been in office long.

When I spoke to Mother Billingsley about the dream, I told her not to resign, and she stated to me that she was not going to resign. *In the later part of 2004, I dreamed again, but this time the Lord showed me she was going to be removed from her position as supervisor* by Bishop J. C. Gilkey. I went back to my son and my sister and told them the second dream. My son was concerned, and I told him that unless the Lord changed His mind, it was going to happen. In other words a *dismissal was going to take place.* I went back to Mother Billingsley after having the second dream and told her if she needed to resign to go ahead and resign. She stated that she had never resigned from anything. After the Lord changed the dream, I did not want her to be embarrassed or hurt. I expressed to her that I felt something was not favorable in her working relationship with the bishop, and I asked her to go and talk to him. She stated that she had the confidence that everything would work out.

I told Mother Gladys Gilkey (the bishop's wife) after I had the second dream that I was going to share with her something that the Lord had showed me, but I would not tell her until after it had taken place. I did not want to contribute to the decision the bishop was going to make as a result of what the Lord had showed me.

On Saturday, June 11, 2005, I was sitting in the credential holders' meeting, the monthly meeting our jurisdiction has with the credential holders of the church—pastors, missionaries, etc. I sat in the meeting expecting the announcement of her removal to be made. After Bishop Gilkey made the announcement, I was hurt for her and also for Bishop Gilkey. The decision appeared to affect him as well as Mother Billingsley. After the meeting I went to the bishop and told him there was nothing he could have done to prevent it because the Lord said she was going to be removed. He then called Pastor Mark Gilkey (his son) for me to tell him what the Lord had said, and I did. Numbers 23:19 says, "God is not a man, that he should lie; neither the son of man, that he should repent: hath he said, and shalt he not do it? Or hath he spoken, and shall he not make it good?"

After I shared with Mother Billingsley what the Lord had showed me, she let me know that she was somewhat devastated after she was removed from the position as supervisor, and she sat down at her computer to write a letter to the national church, but she decided to open her Bible before writing the letter. She opened to the Scripture in Psalm 75:6–7:

> For promotion cometh neither from the east, nor from the west, nor from the south. But God is the judge: he putteth down one, and setteth up another. She further stated because of what the lord had showed her in his word, she did not write the letter.

The Lord allowed her to be dismissed from the position of Kansas southwest supervisor to be appointed to another position as the international president of the Young Women's Christian Council. "God's ways are not our ways."

Daughter Found after Fourteen Years

In 2006, Sister Tina Mayes of Wichita, Kansas, told me that she wanted to see her only daughter, who she had not seen for fourteen years. I told her that I was going to pray that the Lord would bless her to see her daughter. A few weeks later Sister Mays was visiting her mother in Kansas City, who was diagnosed with cancer. She received a message that the father of her daughter was also visiting in Kansas City because his brother-in-law was also diagnosed with cancer. Through some of the family members, they were able to contact each other, and *she was able to see her daughter after fourteen years.* God still answers *in the closet of prayer.*

Daughter Restored Again after Four Years

In 2010, Sister Mayes stated to me again, that she had not seen her daughter since the time of her mother's illness and demise in March 2006, and she did not know where she lived. I told her I was going to pray again that she would see her daughter.

I prayed, and within two or three weeks, she notified me that her niece had located her daughter on Facebook, and she was living in Texas. She further stated that she was able to make connections with the father, but she did not think he was going to let her see her daughter. I told her if the Lord allowed her to find her daughter again, I felt He would bless her to see her, and her daughter's father was not big enough to box with God. A day or so later, if not the same day, she called me and said the father was bringing her daughter to Wichita, Kansas, and she was going get to see her. When she arrived, she called and asked if I would come and meet her, and I did. *God is a revealer and a miracle-working God.*

Son Returned Home

In approximately 1981 or 1982, my son Tony U. Gentry left home, and I was told I would never see him again. I would go to work at Wesley Hospital in Wichita, Kansas, and as I would walk down the halls to patient rooms to do treatments, *I would have a prayer in my heart.* Without saying anything to anyone, I entered one of my patients' rooms to do her morning treatment, having to wear a gown and mask. When I received report on this patient, prior to entering her room, some of the nurses had stated that she appeared to be somewhat confused. Upon entering the room for the first time, without saying a word to the patient, she raised up in the bed, not even knowing my name, *and said, "Anything you ask the Lord, He will do it."*

I paused at the door, and I had to take note because the Lord was speaking to me through this patient who was reported to be confused. I returned to her room again in the afternoon to do another treatment, and as I entered the room the second time, the patient raised up again in the bed and said, *"I said anything you ask."* The Lord used this lady who people thought was confused and somewhat senile to make known the truth of the gospel. A few days later my son returned home, and he is now my pastor.

> But God had chosen the foolish things of the world to confound the wise; and God hath chosen the weak things of the world to confound the things which are mighty: And base things of the world, and things which are despised, God chosen, yea and things which are not, to bring to nought things that are. (1 Cor. 1:27–28)

Testimony of Money Released

> Verily I say unto you whatsoever ye shall bind on earth shall be bound in heaven, and whatsoever ye shall loose on earth shall be loosed in heaven. (Matt. 18:19–20)

When you reach out to others, the Lord will allow blessings to come to you. On December 10, 11, and 12, I went on a three-day fast for the needs of someone else. I had needs of my own, but each time I fast for others, I always receive a blessing. I had a physical and financial need. I wanted to go to Las Vegas to see my youngest son, who I had not seen for a few years, even though I needed the money for other expenses. It came into my spirit that if I purchased an airline ticket for me and my grandson to go to Las Vegas, I would receive money that was denied me in 2011. While in 9:00 a.m. prayer on December 17, 2013, after completing a three-day fast a few days prior, I asked the Lord to allow the money I did not receive to be released. The very hour I was in prayer, I had a missed call on my phone, and after prayer, I played the message back, which came in at 9:50 a.m. The message let me know that the business that had prevented me from receiving the money in 2011 had filed a claim with their insurance company and wanted to send me papers to release the money which I was denied, *and the money was released.* I paid my tithe, paid off my home and car and paid other bills. Isaiah 65:24 says, "And it shall come to pass, that before they call, I will answer, and while they are yet speaking; I will hear." Therefore while I was petitioning God, He was already at work, and the same hour I got a response.

Testimony of Stress Relieved

In the early part of the 1980s, I had a very depressing dream in regard to my oldest son, Tony Gentry. I began to pray and remind the Lord that I taught stress classes and I was in stress myself. I asked the Lord to give me a word, and I opened my Bible to Psalm 107:6, 8: "Then they called unto the Lord in their trouble, and He delivered them out of their distresses. *The Lord lifted the burden.* Oh that men would praise the Lord for his goodness and his wonderful works to the children of men." That Scripture was birthed in my spirit from that day, and I use it frequently, praising God for His goodness and His wonderful works. *The word of God brings deliverance and relieves stress.*

Testimony of Burden Lifted

In 2011, Mother Maretta Pete stated that she was very upset, full of rage, and wanted to harm a man who she felt had done her wrong. She would go to bed angry and wake up angry. On this particular morning, she woke up still upset and full of rage. Then all of a sudden the telephone rang, and it was one of the members of Emanuel Church of God in Christ, Mother Winbush, who asked her if she and I could come for a visit. She responded in the affirmative. We went to her home, witnessed to her about the Lord, read a Scripture, and prayed.

After praying, she stated that she felt the presence of the Lord and felt as though He had given her peace and softened her heart (her burden was lifted), which allowed her to be able to forgive the person who had done her wrong.

When he became ill, she was able to care for him without any remorse and remained with him until his demise. She further stated that it was as if the Lord sent us at the right time, and the phone call changed her life. She surrendered her life to the Lord and became a member of Emmanuel Church, and now she has peace, saying, "What a mighty God we serve." Because of the change in her life, many other people have become members.

Stronghold of Addiction Destroyed

My sister Virginia Burns had a problem smoking, and my sister Missionary Archie went to her mouth and cupped her hands on the outside of her mouth. She took the smoking habit and threw it away as we had family prayer, and *my sister received salvation and was delivered from smoking.*

Reported Drug Users Relocated

In *May 2006* I was told that the people who had moved into the house next door to me were using drugs. I told a neighbor of mind not to worry because I was going to tell the Lord about it, and He would take care of it. When I first prayed, there did not seem to be any changes, so I felt I needed to go witness to them and pray again. I went next door and witnessed to the people and had prayer, and shortly afterward they moved away.

> Therefore I say unto you What things soever ye desire, when you pray, believe that ye receive them, and ye shall have them. (Mark 11:24)

Prophecy of Protection through Obedience

In the week of June 26, 2011, I dreamed I was in a large parking lot, and as I went to my car, it would not start. I tried to use my cell phone, and it would not work. I got out of my car to see if I could use the phone of someone else to call my son. As I got out the car, I had left the driver's door open, and my purse was in the front seat of my car. When I had made the call, I stayed out only briefly after making the call. When I went back to get into the car, I saw about five men, and three of them left and two got into my car. When I woke up out of the dream, I decided that if my car were to stop, I would not leave the door open; I would get in the car and lock the door.

On the night of June 29, 2011, only three days after having the dream, I went to a Walmart Shopping Center, and when I came out of the store and got in my car to leave, my car would not start and the cell phone would not work, as I had dreamed a few days earlier. There were several cars in the parking lot and Walmart was closing because it was around 10:00 p.m. I stopped a lady to use her cell phone since mine seemed to have been cut off. Then I was able to use my phone even though it was beeping.

I eventually got out of my car and stopped a security truck, and the driver said I could use her phone to call AAA if mine would not work. I was able to call AAA, and as I looked back at my car, I had left the driver's door open, and my purse was in the front seat as was in the dream. I immediately got back into the car. I made sure I remained in the car with my car locked and the windows rolled up while waiting on AAA to arrive. After AAA arrived I looked up and there were five young men walking ahead a few feet away from the car as in the dream. I told the AAA driver that I had seen this episode in a dream, but I thank God that I was attentive to the Lord and followed through with what to do. I am reminded of the Scripture that I had opened my Bible to while in prayer after I had asked the Lord to give me a Word. Isaiah 58:11 says, "I will guide you continually." As I stay in the closet of prayer, I have come to know that the Lord will guide you continually, and He has been true to His word.

Life Restored through Divine Intervention

In 1987 while my dad was ill and as his condition began to decline, we would take turns sitting at his bedside. One night while my sister Mother Chrystell Draper, who had been ill, and my cousin Mrs. Leola Wilkerson were sitting with my dad, my sister stopped responding and seemed lifeless. My sister stated later that she died. It was after midnight in the early hours of the morning, and the other members of the family had retired for the night. As my sister lay unresponsive, Mrs. Wilkerson stated she did not know where she was going, but she left the bedroom where my father and sister were, walked in the dark across the dining room and living room and passed through another bedroom, where people were asleep, and came to the far bedroom where I was asleep and woke me up. I had just come off a seven-day fast, and I went to my sister. While *in the closet of prayer,* we began to pray, and my sister began to respond. The doctor was called, and when he arrived she was responding and doing well.

Healing of My Kidneys

On January 17, 2004, the Enemy attacked my body, and my kidneys were trying to stop working. I was in so much pain and unable to use the bathroom until much later. Again on January 24, 2004, I had the same problem with my kidneys, and my daughter-in-law rushed me to the emergency room. They inserted a catheter into my bladder. Even though I had a challenge, I went to prayer on the same evening with the catheter in my bladder without it being noticed. While I was praying, my pastor, Bishop Gilkey, came and laid his hands on me and prayed. I saw a kidney specialist on the next day, January 25, 2004.

On January 27, 2004, while I was on my knees, the Scripture came to me in 2 Corinthians 12:9–10:

> And he (Jesus) said unto me, My grace is sufficient for thee; for my strength is made perfect in weakness, for when I am weak, then I am strong.

When I would attend national church conventions, I would take catheters with me, in the event I would have to use them. I continued to be faithful in the approaching the throne of grace in closet of prayer. I do not know when the Lord healed me, but He completely healed me, and now several years later I am still healed of that condition.

Healing through Praise

St. Mark Church of God in Christ and Agape Fellowship Church of God in Christ merged in 2008. One Sunday morning after the merge while the members were praising and magnifying the Lord, I jumped while the praises were going forth, and a Missionary Sandra Clemons stated "They don't know who they have among us. When you jumped, I was healed."

Chest Pain Healed

On January 7, 2007, Sister Monica Hill had chest pain and stated she was hurting all day on Sunday morning and Sunday night. On Monday, January 8, 2007, she came to morning prayer, and while we were *in prayer, I laid my hands on her, and the pain left.* She later e-mailed me and told me she still had no more pain.

Temperature Reduced to Normal

My granddaughter Cherish Tanae had an elevated temperature above 102 degrees and was lying in the bed. I went to her home and saw her and attempted to pick her up, but she did not want to be disturbed. *I prayed for her and a short time later rechecked her temperature, and it had gone down from 102 degrees to 98 degrees. She got up and began to play.*

Hole in the Back of Eye Healed

One day I was asked to be the prayer leader on the prayer time line. There was a lady on the telephone line from another state who asked for prayer, stating that the doctor had said she had *a hole in the back of her eye.* We began to pray the prayer of faith. She mentioned that she had an appointment with the doctor on the following Wednesday. After she had gone to the doctor and returned to the prayer time line, she stated that *the hole in her eye was healed.*

Headache Healed

In the later part of 2012, I went to see my daughter Michelle Gentry and her twelve- or thirteen-year-old son, Depaul, was in bed. I was told he had a migraine headache. I went in and prayed for him, and he said he was free of pain and got up almost immediately and started playing.

Healing of Neck and Shoulder

On Sunday, August 26, 2012, I called my daughter Michelle, who did not come to church that day. She stated that her back and neck hurt and had been hurting for three days, to the extent that she was unable to extend her head in order to look up. I prayed for her and after I prayed for her the first time, she said she felt better, but the problem had not been resolved. I prayed two more times because I know God is a healer, and on the third time after I prayed, Michelle said she could look up and had no more pain.

> Jesus said unto him, if thou canst believe, all things are possible to him that believeth. (Mark 9:23)

Shoulder Pain and Facial Pain Healed

On August 25, 2012, after we opened service in a district church setting with prayer, I asked if anyone had any pain. Mother Charlene Howard stated that she had *shoulder pain, and it had lasted for two to three days. We prayed for her, and she stated that the pain left.* While we were praying for Mother Howard, a Missionary McClish testified that as she begin to pray along with us, and the pain she had down the side of her face left.

Prophecy of Being Healed as She Goes

During the latter part of July or the first week in August 2011, I dreamed that my sister (Dr. Charlene Hogan), who lives in Virginia and had undergone spinal surgery a year or so prior and was able to move her neck from side to side better, was not able to move her neck well since her surgery. In the dream I was praying for her neck, and I could feel a knot in the back of her neck. I called Charlene and told her the dream, and she stated that she was able to move her neck better. I did not mention the knot.

After I had that dream, I believed I would be sharing a room with her at our next family reunion, which was to take place in Chicago, Illinois, and that her husband was not coming. I did not know at that time whether her husband was coming. Sure enough in August 5, 2011, until August 8, 2011, I did share a room with her and her daughter. I began to pray for her, and as I began to pray, I felt the knot on the back of her neck, like I had felt and seen in the dream. Certainly God is a revealer, and He is a rewarder to those who diligently seek Him. On August 28, 2011, *I dreamed again that my sister was able to move her neck even better than before,* and I called her again and she confirmed what I had dreamed. When I saw her in November 2013, she was doing even better. Luke 17:14b says, "And it came to pass, that, as they went, they were cleansed."

Prophecy of Headache Healed

On April 21, 2012, I went to New Philadelphia Church of God in Christ for jurisdiction prayer, and while praying I asked the Lord to manifest Himself. *While prayer was being made, the Lord revealed to me that He had just healed someone from a migraine-type headache.* After we had finished praying, I asked who came in with a headache, and a Mother Nettie McClennon stood up and said her head was killing her and she kept going in and out of the church because her head was hurting her so bad, *and all of a sudden her headache just stopped.* The Lord did manifest Himself.

Patient out of Coma and off Dialysis

In the first part of 2013, I received a telephone call from one of the members of the Emmanuel Church of God in Christ requesting prayer for her sister, who was in the hospital here in Wichita. The relative *was in ICU and unresponsive.* I went to the hospital and prayed for the patient, and after I had prayed, I told the family I did not know what the Lord was going to do but *I had prayed.* The next day I received a report that the patient's vital signs were better but she was still unresponsive. *I went back and prayed again, and the patient was beginning to respond, but she kept slipping in and out of a semiconscious state and they had placed her on dialysis.* I told the family I was *going to pray that the Lord would take her off dialysis.* Approximately three to four days later, my son, Pastor Gentry, went to see the patient and stated that the patient was sitting up talking.

Two days passed, and I received another call to *pray again for the patient, for she had a stroke and could not walk well* and if I came up she might not know me. *I prayed over the telephone* and waited another couple of days and returned to the hospital. When I entered the room, the patient recognized me and was talking and walking again. *They took her out of the ICU and off dialysis, and she was dismissed home.*

No Leukemia or Bone Cancer Found

In February 2013, I received a call from Missionary Helen Crump asking me to pray for a patient that the doctors thought could possibly have leukemia and was not eating. We prayed for the patient, and she began to eat almost immediately. *She was tested for leukemia and bone cancer. We prayed again, and all the tests came back negative.* The patient was discharged home.

Healing of Digestive System

Missionary Helen Crump was visiting family in Arkansas, and she had a niece there who was experiencing problems with her digestive system. This condition had lasted for an extended period of time, and she was unable to eat. Missionary Crump and other members of the family, along with her niece, had gone to a restaurant to eat. Since the niece was unable to eat, Missionary Crump made a long-distance call to me and stated, "This child can't continue to go on like this." *I prayed for her by telephone and was told that immediately the child began to eat and has been eating ever since.*

No Cancer Found

On November 13, 2013, I received a call from Missionary Helen Crump, and she asked me to pray for a sixty-five-year-old patient who had been diagnosed with cancer in the past and now had a tumor the size of a football. The doctor thought it could be cancerous. I talked to the patient briefly and asked her to put her hand on her stomach as I prayed by telephone. Missionary Crump stated that she put her hand on the patient's stomach also, and I began to pray that when the surgeon did the surgery that the tumor would not be cancerous. Surgery was performed on the next day, November 14, 2013. *I received a report on November 15, 2013, that there was no report of cancer found.* To God be the glory.

In the Season of Winter—December, January, and February

In the natural closet you will find heavy clothing—fully dressed clothing that can be worn to protect our entire bodies, from our head to our feet.

It is the last season of the year, with the shortest of days. Winter is a time of inclement weather when people regard themselves as vulnerable, a time where we may feel uncomfortable, and a time we experience dreary, dark, cold, depressive, gloomy, and icy days.

In the Closet of Prayer in the Winter Years

In the spiritual closet, winter is the last season of our lives. It is a time to rest in the Lord and hold fast to our profession in Christ Jesus. It is time where we have anchored ourselves in the Lord, gripping to that solid rock, not being easily shaken in our faith. We have put on the full armor of God to be fully covered with that spiritual armor. It is a time of knowing that whatever battle we are confronted with in our lives, God is at the helm, and he is the Captain of the ship, "for the battle is not ours; but God's" (2 Chron. 20:15).

It is a time when we have gone through trials, but our past problems and circumstances have brought about present confidence. It is a time when we understand we did not make it this far on our own but by staying in the closet of prayer. We may not be able to run quickly physically, but our spiritual pace has picked up. Therefore we are running so we may obtain eternal life. We are moving slow but staying in the closet of prayer. It is a time we are "coming boldly unto the throne of grace that we may obtain mercy and find grace to help in time of need" (Heb. 4:16).

So whatever the needs are in our lives, we have the confidence that God is going to work out every problem and bring us through victoriously. "We will not cast away our confidence which have a great recompense of reward" (Heb. 10:35).

We will stay in the closet of prayer with unwavering faith. First John 5:14–15 says, "And this is the confidence we have in him, that, if we ask anything according to his will he heareth us: And if we know that he heareth us, whatsoever we ask, we know that we have the petitions that we desired of him," knowing that we will receive a great reward and blessing. We will not only be blessed in this present world, but in this winter season of our lives, our eyes are also focused on a city whose builder and maker is God.

When we think of aging, we usually think of coming to the end of our journey here on earth, but this journey never ends; it just takes on new directions.

So in the winter of our lives, we can be like Anna, the prophetess in Luke 2:37 who served God with fasting and prayers night and day and who remained in the temple in prayer. If we want a prophetic word from the Lord, and for Him to *reveal Himself* to us, we are to remain in the closet of prayer.

In the Winter Years
Prophecies during the Transitional Years

Prophecy 1

Divine leading: In August of 1987, after returning home from a family reunion in Kansas City, it came to me to call back and talk to the families who remained in Kansas City and tell them to spend more time with my father because I did not think he would be live much longer, but I did not follow through. My Father later returned home to Arkansas and was having some problems with his stomach. I told him to go and have tests run, and he followed my advice.

I called my sister (Maxcine Thomas) in Oklahoma City and asked her if she would go with me to see our father, since I did not think he would be here very much longer. We went to see him in September, and while we were attending the home church there in Arkansas, I missed the opportunity of having my father pray for me one last time. We went a couple more times just to be with him.

My father was diagnosed with cancer of the stomach in late August or September of 1987 and died in November of the same year.

In the month of November prior to my father's death, several members of the family went to Nashville, Arkansas, to visit him, and on one of those days in November, the family had prayer and an altar call in the home. During the altar call, my youngest brother, Nathaniel Hill, accepted salvation. My father was very frail and could hardly stand due to his debilitated state. He got out of bed and began to clap and pray with his son as he accepted the Lord as his personal Savior, and he ministered to him, giving him one last message. He stated, *"You have crossed over to a new life, and in this life is eternal life. Hold on."* My son Tony Gentry referenced these words as the motto of his church when he begin pastoring in 2009: "A place to begin new life."

During my dad's illness, the family would take shifts in sitting with him, and when he would be in severe pain and did not want to take any medication, we would pray and the pain would leave and he would go to sleep.

On November 30, 1987, with the family gathered around his bedside in the master bedroom, the Lord called my father from labor to reward. The last scripture I read to my father was John 14:1–3:

> Let not your heart be troubled: ye believe in God, believe also in me. In my father's house are many mansions; if it were not so I would have told you, I go to prepare a place for you, And if I go and prepare a place for you, I will come again and receive you unto myself; that where I am there ye may be also ...

The last words I remember hearing him say were, *"Now, now, Lord,"* as if it was okay for the Lord to call him home.

Prophecy 2

Prophecy of International Bishop: In 1987 on a Sunday afternoon in April, before returned to church for the evening service, I took a nap, and I dreamed that our international presiding leader, *Bishop J. O. Patterson, fell, and I tried to get to him and was unable.* When I arrived at church at around seven o'clock, I met my pastor, Bishop J. C. Gilkey Sr., outside of the church as I was about to enter the sanctuary. (He had just returned from the International Church of God in Christ business meeting in Memphis, Tennessee.) I asked him how Bishop Patterson was, and he stated that he was okay. *I told Bishop Gilkey, about the dream.*

A year later in April of 1988, Bishop J. O. Patterson was planning to attend another business meeting, and he testified that he *had been diagnosed with cancer.* People all over the United States and perhaps in foreign countries were praying for him. *I went back to my pastor, Bishop J. C. Gilkey, and told him that I never saw him get up. Bishop Gilkey stated to me that he wished I had seen him get up.* In 1989 the Lord called our presiding bishop, Bishop J. O. Patterson, home from labor to reward. His work was finished. In the closet of prayer the Lord reveals things that are to come.

Prophecy 3

Prophecy and preparation before demise: On December 1, 2006, I dreamed that we were closing up the family home where my brother, Lee Artis Hill, lived, as if the Lord was going to soon call him home. I called my brother and told him that if he needed apologize to anyone for him to be sure and do that. He begins to praise the Lord after I told him that. He and his first wife had divorced years prior, and he had remarried. I told him if there was forgiveness that needed to be made in regard to past hurts, I wanted him to do it. In 2009 my brother was diagnosed with cancer, and I told him to be sure and ask his first wife to forgive him if he needed to. He told me that I had told him that before and he already had. I then looked back in my prayer journal where the Lord had showed me the dream, and sure enough, I had already told him to do that. Even though he had apologized in the past, he called me a few days later and told me he went and asked her again. On October 10, 2010, the Lord called my brother home, and I stayed at his bedside for the last forty-eight hours of his life, reading the Word and praying.

> The Lord is not slack concerning his promise, as some men count slackness; but is longsuffering to us-ward, not willing that any should perish, but that all should come to repentance. (2 Peter3:9)

Prophecy 4

Instant prophecy of demise: On the night of August 13, 2009, I walked into my home around 9:25 p.m. after returning from church. I walked into the family room, looked at my telephone, and saw that I had a missed call from my nephew Cleo, who lived in California. As I walked to my telephone and looked down at the telephone with Cleo's number on it, I opened my mouth and said, "Willie Jr. just died." Willie Jr. was Cleo's brother, and he lived in Texas. I picked up the telephone and returned the call, and on the other end of the line was Cleo's wife, who answered the telephone by saying the exact words God had spoken to me: "Willie Jr. just died."

Willie Jr. was a police lieutenant. He was teaching a self-defense class at one of the churches in Texas and had a heart attack and died instantly. On August 17, 2009, I told my sister Mother Chrystell Draper what the Lord had showed me, and she said, "As much as you pray, you should not be surprised by what the Lord showed you." *God is a revealer.*

Prophecy 5

Vision of Sister's Demise: On Memorial Day, Monday, May 25, 2009, my son Pastor Tony Gentry and his wife had a barbeque at their home and invited me, but I decided to remain home. While at home as I was sitting in my lounging chair in the family room, I looked up at a picture on my wall of my twelve brothers and sisters, *and the Lord showed me in a vision my sister Missionary Annette Archie Rhodes. He led me to focus on her picture, letting me know He was going to call her home.* I said, "No, not Annette. She is not as old as some of the others." I looked at another sister in the picture who had expired with cancer and it came to me that *she had lost faith.* I said in my spirit that I would call my sister at around 9:30 that night. I did not call, and at approximately eleven o'clock I received a call from a niece

Marie McElroy in Oklahoma City, and she stated Annette and her husband had traveled from Altus, Oklahoma, to Oklahoma City for a doctor's appointment the next day. I immediately thought of the vision, and I told my son Pastor Gentry what I had seen. I said we needed to go to Oklahoma City after finding out the following day that she was going to have surgery.

When we arrived in Oklahoma City on Wednesday, May 27, 2009, she had been admitted to the hospital and was scheduled for surgery on Thursday, May 28, 2009. When we entered the hospital room, she *said, "Pray that my faith doesn't fail."* Again I thought of what the Lord had showed me in the vision.

They did surgery on my sister and found that her stomach was full of cancer. While she was in the recovery room, she told me that the surgery was a big one and that the Lord let her come back to tell us good-bye. I asked her how she knew, and she said she heard them talking. She was later released from the hospital back to Altus, Oklahoma, and received chemotherapy.

On June 12, 2009, I dreamed that my sister, Maxcine Thomas and I went to see my sister and that she was cheerful, Again the Lord showed me in a dream on January 28, 2010, my sister in a casket and that she was preparing herself. I called her and she was in the hospital receiving blood. I told her the Lord had put her on my heart and in my spirit. On Thursday, February 4, 2010, the Lord showed me in another dream that the family was together and I called my sister's name and she was not there.

On June 26, 2010, my sister Maxcine and I did travel to Altus, Oklahoma, for her birthday celebration, thinking this would be the last time we would be able to attend a birthday celebration for her. As I kept dreaming about my sister, I felt this would soon come to pass.

In August 2010, my sister Missionary Rhodes attended our family reunion in Wichita, and the Lord allowed her to help pray and minister to the needs of the people at our church.

On October 27, 2010, my sister Mother Maxcine Thomas and nephew from Oklahoma accompanied me again to Altus, Oklahoma, in a surprise visit to see my sister. When we entered her home, she began to cry, stating that someone loved her. She was extremely happy. One night while she was eating snacks, I noticed that she was not feeling well. She checked her blood sugar and blood pressure and stated that it was high. I began to pray for her, and immediately she began to feel and look better.

As soon as I finished praying, my nephew Terrance Burns stated that while I was praying, his sinuses opened up. Miracles happen when we stay *in the closet of prayer.*

On Thursday, October 28, 2010, as we were preparing to leave, my sister Missionary Rhodes ministered to our nephew, and he received salvation prior to us leaving. This was my sister's last convert. She had won many souls to Christ during her ministry.

On January 1, 2011, I was lying in bed thinking of my sister and that I might write a letter to the family to pray a special prayer for her when later in the day I received a call from my sister Mother Maxcine Thomas that Missionary Rhodes was in the hospital. I gave her a telephone call and told her the Lord had put her on my heart. I told her that the Lord was establishing her and she was preparing herself. She responded in the affirmative and said He was. *She gave me her testimony,* stating that she had fought a good fight and was getting tired. It came to her mind sometimes to go on and be with the Lord, for that was the best place to be—to be with Jesus, with no more heartache and no more pain. She said for me to tell the ones at her funeral that they didn't have to worry or cry. I told her, "I am going to cry now." We both cried and then started back talking. She further stated, "We all have to go whether today or tomorrow." She mentioned how some of the family had received salvation under her ministry. She and I were blessed to travel together for years to church conventions, and she said those were some of the best years of her life.

On January 5, 2011, I went to my church, and in prayer I told the Lord to go see about my sister, for she was in trouble. The next day I went to prayer, and as I prayed, I felt some relief in my spirit. On Saturday, January 8, 2011, my sister Mother Chrystell Draper from Kansas City, Missouri, and I traveled to Altus, Oklahoma, along with other members of the family to see my sister. When we arrived she was sitting in a chair, and we talked and prayed. On Sunday, January 9, 2011, she signed her will while in the hospital. We were to leave on Monday, January 10, 2011, which was the same day they had decided to do another surgery on my sister, but it had snowed in Wichita, and one of the other family member's airplane was delayed, so we decided to stay.

I told one of my sisters there might be a reason why we were staying. I did not tell her the reason, but in my spirit I felt my sister might not make it out of a surgery, even though she was talking and seemed in good spirits. On Monday evening we sang, prayed, and read the Word of God. We sang one song titled, "We've Come This Far by Faith." She begin to sing the verse so beautifully:

> Just the other day I heard a man say, that he did not believe in God's word, but I can truly say the Lord will make a way, and He never failed me yet. Thank God we've come this for by faith leaning on the Lord, trusting in His Holy Word, He never failed me yet.

Her sisters remained at her bedside, along with her husband and one daughter, until they came and got her for surgery. Before going, she stated that she was tired and was ready to go. One of her sons and his wife, Reverend and Mrs. Lathan Archie, who lived out of the city, did not arrive until after they had taken her

119

in the pre-op holding room prior to surgery. As they arrived they began to greet other members of the family who were in the surgery waiting area. I told them to go and see their mother, and they could greet the other family members later because I did not think my sister would make it out of surgery.

My sister had another son who lived in the city, and I had called him to see when he would be off work. When he arrived, I told him to go back and see his mother. The sons as well as the husband and daughter were able to spend some private time with their mother while the hospital waited to have blood available for her in the case of an emergency.

The youngest son, Eddie Archie, decided to go home after he had seen his mother for a period of time and was going to return later. When I saw him at the elevator, I rushed to stop him and told him to go back in and stay with her until she went into surgery. He said he had already told her good-bye. I told him to go back in and let her know he had not left. He did as I directed and went back in with his mother until they took her to surgery. He then proceeded to go home, and before he left I told him if I called him, I wanted him to come back right away, and he said he would.

The family waited in the surgery waiting area until the surgery was completed and the doctor came out and said she went through the surgery, and we could go in to see her after she began to wake up from the anesthesia. Then he left for home.

Not long after the doctor left, someone from the recovery room came and told the family that the doctor was called back because her condition was deteriorating, and she was not responding to any treatment being administered. I called her son to return to the hospital, and he returned immediately. My sister expired a short time later on January 11, 2011. She never made it out of the recovery room. In the closet of prayer, God will reveal to you things that are to come to past.

Prophecy 6

Prophecy of life extended: In the middle to late part of the 1980s, I dreamed that one of the members of one of our sister churches expired. I shared the dream with Missionary S. Clemons, and she stated that he had backslidden (turned back from serving God). There was a revival in progress at one of the churches, and I decided that since he had fallen out of fellowship with God, I could go with him to the altar when the invitation to come to Christ was made, but I didn't.

After I had the dream, approximately three months later he was diagnosed with cancer, and they did not have any treatment in Wichita to treat the type of cancer he had. They had to send him to another state. I called Bishop Gilkey and shared with him the dream, and I told him that I had never told him. The bishop said, "He is going to be all right." I came to know that so many times when the bishop said those words, the person would be all right, but I knew the Lord did not tell me that. The young man lost a considerable amount of weight and could hardly walk around.

One night I went to sleep, and the Lord showed me in another dream that he was dead. Then in the same dream he showed me that he is not dead but critically ill. I then saw the young man put on weight. Once he came to me and said, "Sister Gentry, I never was sick until after you told me you had a dream about me." I told him I had a dream, but I never told him what it was. He remained ill until he expired some years later.

Prophecy 7

Revelation of My Home-going: On September 21, 2011, I dreamed that the Lord had called me home and I was trying to see if I wanted to be buried or have an open casket for my children and if I had enough pictures of myself.

My Lord is God, and I thank Him for loving me and giving me a chance to prepare myself to meet Him in peace when He calls me home.

On September 30, 2011, I dreamed again that the Lord had called me home. In this dream I saw my father and mother, both deceased. I also saw two saints who are still alive and one of my sisters, Mae Francis McElroy. In the dream we were in a meeting, and when the meeting was over, one of the saints left before I did, and I did not see her anymore. When I woke up, I began to wonder if this person would be called home before the Lord called me home, but God is in control. He left on record for us to be ready. In the dream I also saw my former assistant pastor, who is deceased, walking slowly. I tried to catch up with him to go around him, but I woke up before I caught up with him. My sister Mae Frances McElroy, who was in the dream on September 30, 2011, was diagnosed with cancer in August 2013.

On Saturday, October 1, 2011, I dreamed again that I told a friend of mine to let them know at my funeral that I knew that the Lord was going to call me home. During the week of October 2, 2011, I dreamed again that I was making preparation for whenever the Lord would call me home. Several months before I started dreaming about my death, I went to everyone I thought had something against me or if there seemed to be any kind of misunderstanding between us and asked them to forgive me. I was trying to get my spiritual house in order for when time the Lord will call me from labor to reward.

On December 26, 2011 (a Monday), I dreamed I was in a church service and the speaker (who seemed to be a man) put his hand on my stomach and said I had stage 4 cancer. Later in the dream I went up for prayer and (seemingly a lady at this time) stated I had stage 4 vaginal cancer and that I needed to rest. To the readers, *I will say God is in control, and I trust Him with my life.* I ask the Lord to let me live at least until I am seventy years old, but He has the final say. I am now sixty-eight years old, and I had a brother and a sister die at age sixty-eight and one at age forty-five. The others were older. *To God be the glory.* I do not know how soon, but I am going to prepare myself for that day when the Lord will call my name.

So in the winter months, we are not to be shaken in our faith, but we are to stand firm on the foundation Christ has laid for us, knowing that death is not our future; it is just the avenue we have to take to get to our destination (the place called home).

We are positioning ourselves in a state of readiness, looking for that great day and the coming of the Lord. As we go through the different seasons, including spring, summer, and fall, they are preparing us for the winter. As we look back and see how the Lord has blessed us in each season of our lives, we can say the blessings of the Lord makes us rich and add no sorrow to it.

On January 5, 2012, I dreamed that my sister Missionary Annette Archie Rhodes, who is deceased, came and took me by the hand. I have done like Hezekiah in the book of Isaiah 38:1 and 2 Kings 20:1, when Isaiah told Hezekiah that the Lord said, "Set thine house in order; for thou shalt die and not live." Hezekiah made supplication to God in prayer; then the Lord went back to Isaiah and said to tell him he would add to his life fifteen more years.

In the event that the Lord does not extend my life as I would like, I have tried to prepare my family, and I tell the Lord that if I am ready, when He decides to call me home, I do not want to suffer. I want to just go to sleep, but while I am in this tabernacle (body), I must work the work of Him who sent me while it is day (while I am able) because the time will come when I won't be able to work anymore.

> Yea I think it meet as long as I am in this tabernacle,
> to stir you up by putting you in remembrance.
> Knowing that shortly I must put off this my

tabernacle, even as our Lord Jesus Christ hath
shewed me. (2 Peter 1:13–14)

On June 26, 2012, while I was on a consecration, I was
awake, asleep, or in a trance, and *I saw a light brighter than any
light I had ever seen. It seemed crystal clear, radiant, and beautiful.* I
felt peace and happiness. I then came out of it. What a glorious
appearance and experience. I shared the experience with my son
Pastor Gentry and other members of my family.

Consolation from God

On May 27, 2013, the Lord showed me in a dream or trance
that *He would be with me always, even in troubled times.* That gave
me comfort. When I went to church for morning prayer, that
thought lingered with me, and I am reminded of Psalm 23:4,
which says, "Yea though I walk through the valley of the
shadow of death, I will fear no evil; for thou art with me; thy
rod and thy staff they comfort me."

Medical Report

On August 8, 2013, I went to the Wichita surgical specialist,
and I received a report in the mail. Under the "Problem List"
was, "CA of Female Breast." Under the impression from a CT
scan was, "Right Paratracheal Lymph Node" (a lymph node
about one inch in size on the outside of my trachea), which is
concerning of metastatic disease (cancer that has spread) due to
the mammogram of my breast, which was obtained the same
day. It also said, "Plan: Recommended a percutaneous needle
core breast biopsy, but that Pauline [I] would not like to proceed.
She has decided she does not want to have any treatment if the
area is cancer and would like to leave the process on the disease
in God's hands."

After the above report, I remain encouraged in the Lord, more at this stage of my life than I have ever been. I am continuing the work of the Lord and staying in the closet of prayer, knowing I must work the work of Him who sent me while it is day, for the time will come when I will not be able to work anymore.

On August 12, 2013, I began to think about the words given me from the Lord on May 27, 2013, that "He would never leave me nor forsake me." I opened my Bible to Deuteronomy 31:6: "Be thou strong and of a good courage, Fear not, nor be afraid of them, for the Lord thy God, he it is that doth go with thee, He will not fail thee nor forsake thee." Isaiah 38:15 says, "What shall I say? He hath both spoken unto me, and himself hath done it: I shall go softly all my years."

Whether two years, three years, or five years, I just want to hear the Lord say, "Well done, thou good and faithful servant … enter thou into the joy of the Lord" (Matt. 25:21).

Therefore in the winter months we have complete confidence in God and yield to His will, knowing that it is well with our soul. When He speaks, we can repeat the words of the song by Andrae Crouch that says, *"God has spoken, let the church say amen."*

Workshop on How to Prepare to Enter the Closet of Prayer

Prayer Workshop Outline

President: Mother Pauline Gentry

1. Effectual fervent prayer: James 5:16. Outline for discussion.

    _____

    _____

2. Definition of prayer—communication with God.

    _____

    _____

3. How to pray—pray with humility, pray with sincerity, pray in faith with expectation.

    _____

    _____

4. Closet of prayer—personal conversation between you and God.

    _____

    _____

5. Hindrances of prayer—known sin, insincerity, unbelief, refusing to forgive.

    _____

    _____

6. Effects of prayer—brings victory, humility, results.

_____

_____

7. Fasting with prayer—loose the bands of wickedness, undo heavy burdens, let the oppressed go free, and break every yoke.

_____

_____

8. Unity in prayer—two or three touching as agreeing.

_____

_____

9. Position of prayer—no specific position; it is the heart that counts.

_____

_____

10. Prayer directives for a specific need or condition.

_____

_____

Scriptures

James 5:16: "The effectual fervent prayer of a righteous man availeth much."

As we complete this workshop, I hope that each of us avail ourselves to the repeated command of God. 1Thessalonians 5:17, 25; Romans 12:12; Colossians 4:2; 1Timothy 2:8

Principles of Prayer Workshop

1. Prayer avails when made fervently and earnestly.

2. Prayer avails when we enter into the closet and are shut in that secret place where communication is between you and God (Matt. 6:6, Ps. 91:1).

3. Prayer avails when made in faith (Gen. 12:7–8, 15:1–6; Matt. 17:20; James 1:6–7; Heb. 11:6).

4. Prayer avails when prayed in the name of Jesus (John 14:6, 13–4; Col. 3:17).

5. Prayer avails when made in the will of God (Matt. 26:39; 2 Cor. 12:7–9; 1 Cor. 5:1–5; 1 John 5:14).

6. Prayer avails when made by a supplicant who has confessed and renounced sin (Ps. 51:1–3, 66:18; Prov. 28:9, 13; 1 John 3:8–9; Rom. 6:1; 1 John 2:1–3; Luke 15:18).

7. Prayer avails when made with a forgiving heart (James 5:14–16; Matt. 6:12–15).

8. Prayer avails when made with the right attitude, unselfishly, and with thanksgiving (Gen. 3:1–7; James 1:2, 4:3; 1 Tim. 2:1–3; Phil. 4:6; Ps. 37:4–5).

Workshop Lesson

Theme: Women of prayer, wisdom, and courage

Topic: Prayer that avails much

Lesson Scripture: 1 Samuel 1:9–15, 26–28, 2:1, James 5:16

Key Verse: "The effectual fervent prayer of a Righteous man (woman) availed much" (James 5:16).

Definition of Key Words

1. **Prayer:** A sincere utterance from the heart, communication with God.
2. **Effectual:** A prayer that brings results.
3. **Fervent:** A prayer that is intense, passionate, with great feeling.
4. **Availeth:** A prayer that accomplishes much and brings victory.

Body of the Lesson

One of the most powerful subjects in the Bible is prayer. Prayer is the sincere desire and adoration of God (Rom. 10:1). Prayer is spiritual armor for the saints. It serves as a defensive covering of protection. Prayer is the preparation for danger. It sets miracles in motion. It is the vehicle of communication that helps us access heaven. No sinner can be saved without prayer, and no believer can be sanctified without prayer. It is the key that channels us to unlock the doors of heaven, giving us spiritual insight and directing us through ways to accomplish the task at hand

Reference Scripture: 1 Samuel 1:1–28

Hannah (Grace) was a praying woman who was barren. She was married to Elkanah (God's chosen), who was a righteousness man. He was an Ephrathite of the tribal territory of Ephraim. Elkanah had a second wife named Penniah who had children, but Hannah had no children and was provoked by her adversary because the Lord had closed her womb. Therefore she wept and did not eat because she was miserable and destitute, and only God could give her the joy she desired. Hannah didn't just sit idly and complain about her situation, but she exercised her faith in God through prayer.

Through Hannah's desperation, submission, and contrite spirit, she grew closer to God, and in her misery she trusted in God's true grace. She entered into the closet of prayer and drew apart from her adversary to commune with God. Her prayer was accomplished by the vow that if God would give her a son, she would give him back to Him for the rest of his life. She further vowed he would be a Nazarite (Num. 6:1–4) and would separate himself to the Lord. Hannah remembered God and kept her vow. "Better is it that thou shouldest not vow than that thou shouldest vow and not pay" (Eccles. 5:5).

Regardless of the circumstances, Hannah continued to pray before God. Hannah's prayer was intense, completely spiritual, and inward, for she spoke from the heart. She travailed in prayer, pouring out her soul before the Lord. The petition Hannah made was fervent as well as sincere, and God granted her request. *"The effectual fervent prayer of a righteous man availed much" (James 5:16).*

Hannah was the elect of God, and the Lord avenged her of the adversary, the Devil, because of her continual sincere prayer made to Him. Hannah was misunderstood by Eli (the priest), who marked her mouth, and even though he thought she was drunk, she continued to consult God in prayer. She did not stop praying even after God had granted her request, but she continued to pray and rejoice in the Lord. Hannah prayed and said, "My heart rejoiceth in the Lord, mine horn [strength] is exalted in the Lord: My mouth is enlarged over mine enemies; because I rejoice in thy salvation" (1 Sam. 2:1).

We are the Hannahs of today. We are chosen women of God seeking Him for direction in whatever challenges we are faced with, knowing God will answer the effectual fervent prayer of a righteous man or woman. Just as Hannah entered into her closet of prayer, the Lord commissioned me to enter into the closet of prayer in the church, helping me to realize that an effectual fervent prayer accomplishes much.

I am reminded of a song that one of the international bishops of the Church of God in Christ sang. "Don't stop praying, the Lord is nigh. Don't stop praying, He will hear your cry. The Lord has promised, His Word is true. Don't stop praying, He'll answer you."

It takes the power of prayer for liberation to take place in those who have been bruised and need comforting, injured and need to be restored, and wounded and need to be mended. It takes the power of prayer for the captive to be delivered and those who are bound by satanic forces to be set free. It takes the power of prayer for the brokenhearted to be healed and to help the ones who have been overcome or plagued with grief or despair.

It takes the power of prayer for the blind to recover sight (to regain what was lost), whether physically blind or having lost direction by being disconnected from God.

Discussion Starters

1. What is prayer?
2. What is the closet of prayer?
3. Do you think Hannah entered into the closet of prayer?
4. Why do you think the Lord answered Hannah's prayer?
5. Name some hindrances to prayer.

Prayers of Thanksgiving, Deliverance, Salvation, Healing and Praise

Prayer of Thanksgiving

Lord, in the name of Jesus we thank You for another day—a day You allowed us to see, for this is the day that You have made, and we are rejoicing and being glad in it.

We thank You for Your love—the love You have shown toward us by giving Your life that we may live. As 1 John 15:13 says, "Greater love hath no man than this that a man lay down his life for his friend."

Lord, we thank You for not only dying on the cross, but on the third day You rose from the grave, with all power in Your hand. Revelation 1:18 says, "I am he, that liveth, and was dead, and behold I am alive for ever more, Amen, and hold the keys of hell and of death." So Lord, we thank You. We thank You for Your outstretched hand being extended to all who will open up their hearts and let You come in and receive salvation.

First Thessalonians 4:16–17 says, "So when the Lord himself shall descend from heaven with a shout, with the voice of the Archangel and with the Trump of God and the dead in Christ shall rise first. Then we which are alive and remain shall be caught up together with them in the clouds to meet the Lord in the air. So shall we ever be with the Lord." Therefore we thank You.

We thank You for Your mercy because it is of Your mercy that we are not consumed, because Your compassion fails not. It is new every morning, and great is Your faithfulness toward us.

We thank You for Your grace, that unmerited favor that can only come from You. We don't know how to thank You as we should, but from the depths of our hearts, we say thank You.

We thank You for a thanksgiving of praise—a praise that is in our hearts for the many blessings You have bestowed upon us. Psalm 107:8 says, "Oh that men would praise the Lord for his goodness and for his wonderful works unto the children of men," so, Lord, we lift up our hands with our hearts to You, giving You thanks because You are worthy of the praise.

So today we give thanks unto the Lord, for He is good, His mercy is everlasting, and His truth endures to all generations, and we are entering into Your gates with thanksgiving and into Your courts with praise, realizing the grave can't praise You and death can't celebrate You. So while I live, I am going give You praise. Therefore we are going to be thankful to You and bless Your holy name.

Lord, we thank You for the precious gift of the Holy Ghost— that precious gift that dwells down on the inside of us, to lead us and guide us in all truth. That gift keeps us from yielding to the Enemy. Lord, in every situation of our lives we are going to give You thanks. In 2 Thessalonians 5:18, You said in everything for us to give You thanks, for this is Your will concerning us, and for this we give You thanks. *Amen.*

Prayer of Deliverance

Lord, we come humbly before Your throne of grace so we may obtain mercy and find grace to help in the time of need (Heb. 4:16). Lord, we need Your deliverance power.

You said cast our cares on You for You care for us, for Your yoke is easy and Your burden is light. Lord, lift burdens.

Let the oppressed go free. Give relief to the fatherless and the widows. Relieve the distressed in our homes. Relieve distresses on our jobs. Relieve the distresses of our minds, and give us Your peace. You said in Isaiah 26:3, "You will keep us in perfect peace whose mind is stayed on thee." Help us to focus our minds on You. Help us to focus our thoughts on You and surrender to Your will. Give us the mind of Christ, who walked not after the flesh but after the Spirit. Destroy the yokes. Let deliverance come. David said in Psalms 34:17, "The righteous cry and the Lord heareth, and delivered them out of all their troubles."

Give us strength to go through our troubles and endure trials as good soldiers in Christ Jesus. We are troubled on every side, but Paul said in 2 Corinthians 4:8 we are troubled yet not distressed, knowing in 2 Corinthians 4:17 that "our light afflictions are only but for a moment but it worketh for us a far more exceeding weight in glory." Psalm 34:19 says, "Many are the afflictions of the righteous but you will deliver us out of them all." So let Your deliverance come, and let Your will be done in our lives. Lord, I surrender to Your will, for You know what is best for us. So, Lord, let deliverance come.

We know You can deliver us from the hand of the Enemy. Your Word says in Isaiah 59:19. "When the enemy shall come in like a flood the spirit of the Lord shall lift up a standard against him." So empower us with Your Spirit so we may rise above the storms in our lives to be able to stand against the wiles or tactics of the Devil. Then we will be able to count it all joy when we fall into different temptations.

As we go through our trials, we are going to praise You, for Psalm 33:1 says, "Praises are comely for the upright." It is only the natural thing for us to do, knowing You are a deliverer. So in everything we give You thanks, realizing this is Your will concerning us. Help us to accept Your will and keep believing You for deliverance, for You said no good thing will

You withhold from those who walk upright. Whatever we go through, help us to remember that in the end it will be a good thing. For this we pray. *Amen.*

Prayer of Salvation

Lord, we thank You for Your mercy and Your grace. We thank You for extending Your hand of salvation. You said in Your Word in Acts 2:21, "Whosoever shall call upon the name of the Lord shall be saved." "For neither is their salvation in any other and there is none other name under heaven given among men whereby we must be saved" (Acts 4:12), and that is by Your name. So Lord, save us.

We are seeking You for salvation. You said if we seek You we shall find You if we search for You with our whole hearts. Lord, we are seeking You today, our hearts are open unto You. We are not only seeking You for ourselves, but we are also seeking You so You will draw others unto You. Lord, You are no respecter of persons. You came so this world may be saved. Lord, You loved us so and said in John 3:16, "For God so loved the world, that He gave his only begotten Son, that whosoever believeth in him should not perish, but have everlasting life."

You said the Lord takes pleasure in His people, and He will beautify the meek with salvation. Lord, we are Your people and the sheep of Your pasture. Isaiah 55:6 says, "Seek ye the Lord while he may be found, call ye upon him while he is near." According to Romans 10:8–9, Your word is near to us, "for it is (Nigh) thee, even in thy mouth and in thy heart; that is the word of faith, which we preach. That if thou shalt confess with thy mouth the Lord Jesus and believe in thine heart that God hath raised him from the dead, thou shalt be saved." So Lord, we are believing You today, not only for ourselves but for our children. So save us today, Lord, and save our children. Paul and Silas said in Acts 19, "Believe on the Lord Jesus and thou shalt be saved and thy household." Lord, we know You can not only save our children, but You can also save our entire household. So Lord, save today.

Acts 3:19 says, "Repent ye therefore and be converted, that Your sins may be blotted out, when the times of refreshing shall come from the presence of the Lord." We know if we call on Your name out of a clean heart, we shall be saved. So Lord, we are asking You to clean our hearts. According to Psalm 51, blot out our transgressions, wash us thoroughly from our iniquity, and cleanse us from our sin. Lord, create in us a clean heart, O God, and renew a right spirit within us. Restore unto us the joy of Thy salvation, and uphold us with Thy free Spirit. Then we can teach transgressors Thy ways, and sinners shall be converted unto Thee. *Amen.*

Prayer for Healing

Lord, I thank You this day, a day when we can come humbly before You asking for Your healing power. You said in 2 Chronicles 7:14, "If my people which are called by my name shall, humble themselves, and pray, and seek my face, and turn from their wicked ways; then will I hear from heaven, and will forgive their sin, and will heal their land." Lord, we are Your people, and we are calling on Your name.

So Lord, we come humbly before You, seeking Your face for healing, and if there is any iniquity in our hearts, Lord, we ask You to forgive us, for we don't want our prayers hindered. Lord, we thank You for Your healing power and for being the I am God as in Exodus 15:26: "For I am the Lord that healeth thee."

So I thank You for Your healing power. In Jeremiah 30:17 you said, "For I will restore health unto thee and will heal thee of thy wounds saith the Lord." So Lord, restore us and make us whole by Your healing virtue. Lord, we know there is nothing too hard for You, so Lord, deliver us from these afflictions and heal us from all manner of diseases.

James 5 says, "If any afflicted among you let him pray," so Lord, we are praying for healing, for we know You are able to do exceeding abundantly, above all we can ask or think according to the power that works in us. So Lord, work through us and work with us, and let Your healing take place within us.

James also said if any sick among you, let him call for the elders of the church, and let them pray over him and the prayer of faith shall save the sick. So Lord, we are standing on Your promises, and we are petitioning You earnestly in prayer because the effectual fervent prayer of a righteous man avails much. So Lord, we are walking upright before You, and we are speaking the truth in our hearts; therefore, Lord, hear us when we pray.

In Mark 11:24, You said whatever things we desire when we pray, we must believe we will receive them and we shall have them. So Lord, increase our faith to believe Your every word. Remove all doubt so we may be steadfast in believing Your healing word.

Lord, we know You are able to heal and deliver, for You made the heavens and the earth by Your power and stretched-out arms, and there is nothing too hard for You. So Lord, let Your healing begin, be merciful to us, and give us patience to wait on Your healing, for we trust You. Psalm 57:1 says, "Be merciful unto me O God, be merciful unto me: for my soul trusteth in thee: yea, in the shadow of thy wings will I make my refuge, until these calamities be overpast."

So Lord, as it says in Psalm 31:1, "In Thee, O Lord do I put my trust, let me never be ashamed: deliver me in thy righteousness. For Lord You were wounded for our transgressions, You were bruised for our iniquities: the chastisement of our peace was upon You and with Your stripes we are healed."

So Lord, will You heal us today? Let Your eyes be open and Your ears be attentive to the prayer that is made in this place.

As it says in 2 Chronicles 7:15, "For your ear is not too heavy that you cannot hear us," and You said in Matthew 7:7, "Ask and it shall be given." So Lord, we are asking.

John 14:13–14 says, "And whatsoever ye shall ask in my name, that will I do that the Father may be glorified in the Son. If ye shall ask anything in my name, I will do it." So Lord, we are asking You to let Your healing take place, from the tops of our heads to the soles of our feet. Heal the mind, heal the body, heal the soul, and heal the spirit in Your name, Jesus. *Amen.*

Prayer of Praise

Lord, we thank You for Your kindness, for Your tender mercy, for Your love, and for another day that we can Praise You,

Psalms 147 says, "It is a good thing to give praises unto the Lord Most High. It is a good thing to sing praises, for praises are comely [lovely, pleasant] for the upright, for the saints, those set apart for the Master's use."

We are going to leave all other agendas behind, coming today with one purpose in mind, and that is to praise You. Lord, clear our minds and our thoughts as we lift up our hearts with our hands to You, God.

We praise You for Your love shown toward us that while we were yet sinners You died for us, You saved us, and You canceled all our debts and rescued us from this world of sin and from ourselves.

Hebrews 13:15 says, "Let us offer the sacrifice of praise, for your sacrificial death, giving you praise as we lift up your name." You said in Your Word, "If I be lifted up, I will draw all men unto Me," and for this we give You praise.

Psalm 107: 32 says, "Let us exalt him also in the congregation of the people, praise him in the assembly of the elders." Psalm 148:12–13 says, "Both Young men, and maidens, old men and children. Let them Praise the Name of the Lord for his name is excellent." There is no name higher than Your name. Therefore, Lord, we are going to give You praise. We are going to praise You individually, and we are going to praise You collectively.

As we praise You in the sanctuary, we are going to praise You for Your mighty acts. We are going to praise You according to Your excellent greatness. We are going to praise You with the sound of the trumpet. We are going to praise You with the timbrel and dance. You said let everything that has breath praise the Lord. Praise the Lord.

Whatever problem we have, we are going to lift up our hands with our eyes and heart toward heaven, and give You praise. We praise You that yokes will be broken. We praise you that burdens will be lifted because you said in Isaiah 10:27, "The yoke shall be destroyed because of the anointing."

We are not going to wait until this battle is over to give You praise. We are going to praise You now. We know the Devil does not want us to praise You, but while we live, we are going to give You praise, for the grave can't praise You, and death can't celebrate You. The living shall praise You, as we do this day.

So Lord, we give You praise both now and forever. Praised be the name of the Lord. Amen.

One-Line Meditations or One-Line Prayers

1. Lord, I love You, and I adore You.

2. Lord, I thank You, for You have been so good.

3. Lord, You have been better to me than I have been to myself.

4. Lord, forgive me. Create within me a clean heart.

5. Lord, renew the right spirit within me.

6. Lord, draw me closer to You because I want to be more like You.

7. Lord, help me. I can't make it without You.

8. Lord, I'm leaning and depending on You.

9. Lord, I put my trust in You. There is no other help I know.

10. Lord, help us today. Help us to do Your will.

11. Lord, not as I will, but Thy will be done.

12. Yes, Lord. Yes to Your will. Yes to Your way.

13. Lord, we give You glory. Let Your glory be revealed.

14. Come in my heart, Lord, and move by Your power.

15. Lord, rest in me, rule in me, and abide in me.

On February 1, 2012, after I prayed for one to three hours, the Lord gave me a song, which follows.

Song Given to Me While in Prayer

Just To Be in Your Presence

Just to be in Your presence, just to be in Your presence, just to be in Your presence, in the presence of the Lord.

I found joy in Your presence, I found joy in Your presence, I found joy in Your presence, in the presence of the Lord.

I found peace in Your presence, I found peace in Your presence, I found peace in Your presence, in the presence of the Lord.

I found love in Your presence, I found love in Your presence, I found love in Your presence, in the presence of the Lord.

Message 1
By Mother Pauline Gentry

The Clarion Call
An Urgent Call for action

Thus saith the Lord of host, consider ye and call for the mourning women, that they may come; and send for cunning women, that they may come. And let them make haste and take up a wailing for us, that our eyes may run down with tears, and our eyelids gush out with waters. (Jer. 9:17)

I will therefore that men pray everywhere, lifting up holy hands, without wrath and doubting. (1 Tim. 2:8)

We are commissioned to answer the clarion call. It's a call given by God—a call to pray. Everybody can't answer the call; it's for those who have been called by God. It's for the cunning (clever and skillful) men and women who have surrendered their lives to God.

Jeremiah 9:17 says, "Thus saith the Lord of hosts, Consider ye, and call for the mourning women, that they may come; and send for cunning women, that they may come." We are living in perilous times (times of trouble, times of danger, times of distress and darkness). We need to pray as never before.

In these times we hear of wars and rumors of wars (wars in Iraq, wars in Iran, wars in Afghanistan, wars in the streets of our cities, wars in our homes, wars in the churches, and wars in our own minds). Matthew 24:6 says, "And ye shall hear of wars and rumors of wars: see that ye be not troubled: for all things must come to pass, but the end is not yet."

False prophets (pretenders of the gospel) will deceive many, and if it were possible, they would fool the very elect (saints of God). Matthew 24:11 says, "And many false prophets shall rise, and deceive many." We are living in times where the love of many has grown cold because iniquity has abounded. (My mother, Missionary Alice Hill, used to say, "Love is low sick.") It's a time where many shall be offended and will betray one another for prestige, lack of recognition, or a position. The underlying cause is because of the sin.

We look at nation against nation. One nation wants to be superior and look good in the eyes of the other. There are earthquakes in divers places.

Matthew 24:7–8 says, "For nation shall rise against nation, and kingdom against kingdom: and there shall be famines, and pestilences, and earthquakes in dives places. All these are the beginning of sorrow." People losing their lives, and some don't even know God. They have no money and no jobs. Morals are on the decline, with laws being passed contrary to the laws of God.

Can you see *the urgency of the call?*

Perilous Times

There are burnings throughout the Land (sometimes set intentionally just for the thrill of it). There is competition in government, in our homes, and sometimes in our churches. Men, being lovers of their own selves (what can I do to promote me?), seemingly forget to realize that, "Promotion cometh neither from the East, nor from the West, nor from the South, But God is the Judge; He putteth down one and setteth up another" (Ps. 75:6).

In these perilous times, people are without natural affection. Men love men, and women love women. They are lovers of pleasure more than lovers of God. We are not thinking on the God who loved us so much that He gave His life for us and created us for His glory. There is *an urgent clarion call to pray.*

There is pornography in the homes (genuine love for one another is on the decline). Children are against parents and parents against children. Children are killing parents, and parents are killing children. Parents are giving children drugs and selling them for drugs and sex. (Can't you see the need for the call?)

Luke 12:53 says, "The father shall be divided against the son, and the son against the father; the mother against the daughter, and the daughter against the mother; the mother-n-law against her daughter-n-law, and the daughter-n-law against her mother-n-law."

Parents are babysitting their homes for fear of children taking things out of their homes while they are away. "But except the Lord keep the city, the watchman waketh but in vain" (Ps. 127:1b). It is vain (useless) for you to rise up early, to sit up late, and to eat the bread of sorrows, for the Lord gives His beloved sleep.

In These Perilous Times, There Is a Clarion Call for the Saints

Jeremiah 9:17 says, "Thus saith the Lord of hosts [the I Am That I Am God, said] consider ye [people of God, the ones who have been set apart and chosen, God's elect, see the condition of the people] and call for the mourning women that they may come, and send for cunning women that they may come, and answer the call to pray."

Men and women of God are chosen to walk worthy of the vocation wherewith we are called. We have been summoned to pray, lifting up holy hands with our hearts toward heaven, knowing God is going to hear us. Psalm 34:15 says, "The eyes of the Lord are upon the righteous, and his ears are open unto their cry." He is listening for us, and whatever our petition is, Jesus is on the right hand of the Father making intercession for us. He said in Jeremiah 33:3a, "Call unto me and I will answer thee." We do not know how the Lord will answer, but He said for us to call, and He will answer in His own time and in His own way, for His ways are not our ways, and neither are His thoughts our thoughts. Since we know the Lord has our best interests at heart, we are going to submit to His will, and His will for us is to pray. He has commissioned us to pray without ceasing. We must answer the clarion call until shackles are loosed, until burdens are lifted, until bodies are healed, until people are set free, and until souls are saved.

Message 2
By Mother Pauline Gentry

The Effectual Fervent Prayer of God's People

The effectual fervent prayer of a righteous man availeth much. Elias was a man subject to like passions as we are, and he prayed earnestly that it might not rain; and it rained not on the earth by the space of three years and six months. And he prayed again, and the heaven gave rain, and the earth brought forth fruit. (James 5:16b–18)

The effectual prayer is a prayer that reaches heaven and gets things accomplished. Fervent means intense, earnest prayer from a sincere heart (a heart that is broken, realizing we are helpless without God). It is a heart that is humble before God and believing God will fulfill His promise.

Humble yourselves therefore under the mighty hand of God, that he may exalt you in due time. Casting all your care upon Him; for he careth for you. (1 Peter 5:6–7)

Praying and fasting help us to stay humble before God. Elijah was a man who has passions (emotions, feelings the same vulnerabilities and weaknesses), just as we do. Sometimes in our weaknesses we may not always pass the test, just as Elijah when he fled from the wicked Queen Jezebel when she wanted to destroy his life (1 Kings 19:3). But even in his weaknesses, God was still with him, for He promised never to leave or forsake those who love Him. God worked on Elijah's behalf, and God will work on our behalf and in our favor when our lifestyle supports our prayer life. This confirms that the effectual fervent prayer of a righteous man or woman avails much.

He [Elijah] poured himself into it, put his face between his knees and prayed with Fervor. (1 Kings 18:42)

He may have had his face between his knees, but he had his heart toward heaven. He humbled himself before God, not so much in the position of the body the position of the heart. In Mark 11:22 Jesus said, "Have faith in God." Mark 11:24 says, "Therefore I say unto you what things so ever ye desire when you pray, believe that ye receive them and ye shall have them [not might but shall have them]." Elijah prayed earnestly that it would not rain, and it did not rain for three years and six months. He prayed again, and heaven gave rain and earth produced fruit. Prayer produces fruit, Prayer has lasting benefits.

First Kings 19:41 says, "Elijah said unto King Ahab, get thee up, eat and drink for there is Abundance of rain." When Elijah got through praying, he told his servant to go look toward the sea, and the servant looked and said, "There is nothing." Sometimes we may not see any results when we first pray, but keep on praying and look again. Elijah told the servant to look again seven times, and on the seventh time the servant said, "Behold [look] there ariseth a little cloud out of the sea like a man's hand."

Sometimes when we pray, we may not get the outcome we want right away. We pray for healing and get a little bit better but not the results we want; pray again. We pray for our husband or loved one to receive salvation, and it may take a while; pray again. We pray for finances and get some money but not enough to take care of our needs; pray again.

Elijah told Ahab, "Prepare thy chariot and get thee down that the rain stop thee not," or in other words, prepare for the blessing. Prayer prepares us for a blessing from God. We don't know when the blessing is coming, but pray again, for the effectual fervent prayer of a righteous man avails much.

Author

Evangelist Missionary Mother Pauline Gentry serves as president of the Kansas Southwest Church of God in Christ Jurisdiction Prayer Ministry in Wichita, Kansas. This ministry is composed of pastors and members of forty churches. Her duties with the prayer ministry include visiting the churches throughout the jurisdiction weekly and keeping them encouraged through prayer.

She is a member of her son's church, Emmanuel True Unto God Worship Center Church Of God In Christ, where she coordinates prayer, serves as church mother and the Christian Women's Council president, as well as helps in other areas, with one being evangelizing those who are in need of salvation.

Mother Gentry serves also on the district level in her jurisdiction as president of the advisory board and the evangelist elect lady of the Evangelist Department.

She is the proud mother of two biological children and three adopted children, and she has nine grandchildren and one great-grandchild. Her motto is, "If I can help somebody as I travel along, then my living will not be in vain."

Oh that men would praise the Lord for his goodness, and for his wonderful works to the children of men! (Ps. 107:8)

Contact Information
Mrsgentryinprayer@yahoo.com

CPSIA information can be obtained at www.ICGtesting.com
Printed in the USA
LVOW06s1153060614

388812LV00001B/98/P